Gail Sher Poetry and Poetics 1980-2020

## Also by Gail Sher

PROSE

*One Continuous Mistake: Four Noble Truths for Writers*
*Poetry, Zen and the Linguistic Unconscious*
*The Intuitive Writer*
*From a Baker's Kitchen*

POETRY

*Mary's Eyes*
*Pale Sky*
*Sunny Day, Spring*
*Mingling the Threefold Sky*
*The Twelve* Nidānas
*Figures in Blue*
*The Bardo Books*
*White Bird*
*Mother's Warm Breath*
*The Tethering of Mind to Its Five Permanent Qualities*
*The Haiku Masters: Four Poetic Diaries*
*though actually it is the same earth*
*East Wind Melts the Ice*
*DOHĀ*
*redwind daylong daylong*
*Once There Was Grass*
*RAGA*
*Look at That Dog All Dressed Out in Plum Blossoms*
*Moon of The Swaying Buds*
*Marginalia*
*la*
*KUKLOS*
*Cops*
*Broke Aide*
*Rouge to Beak Having Me*
*(As) on things which (headpiece) touches the Moslem*
*From another point of view the woman seems to be resting*

# Gail Sher
## *Poetry & Poetics*
### 1980–2020

●

NIGHT CRANE PRESS

in collaboration with
The Poetry Collection of the University Libraries
University at Buffalo

2 0 2 0

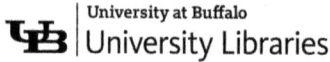

Night Crane Press
in collaboration with
The Poetry Collection of the University Libraries,
University at Buffalo, The State University of New York

University at Buffalo
**UB | University Libraries**

Library of Congress Control Number: 2020901141
Author: Sher, Gail, 1942-
Title: Gail Sher Poetry and Poetics, 1980-2020
Includes bibliographic references.

ISBN: 978-0-9978313-3-7

For Brendan

# CONTENTS

NEW POEMS

Introduction 613

from *City of Sleep* 614

CHRONOLOGIES

# Preface

"My biggest responsibility to myself as a poet is to remain in the realm of the unknown. I don't write what I already know . . . My writing arises, and I am constantly surprised by it."

—Gail Sher, from *Poetry, Zen and the Linguistic Unconscious* (2016)

Bringing together four decades of her writing, *Gail Sher Poetry & Poetics, 1980–2020* is an impressive testament to Gail Sher's ongoing engagement with poetry as a practice of *attention*. It also emphatically reinforces her contributions to, on the one hand, a long tradition of American writing, especially from the West Coast, that is steeped in East Asian philosophy and poetic forms, and, on the other, an equally rich history of experimental writing by women.

Central to Gail Sher's life and work has been her training in Zen, Tibetan Buddhism, and Yoga. After gravitating towards music as a young girl and completing undergraduate and graduate study in English and Middle English, Sher began sitting zazen at the Berkeley Zendo in 1968. Two years later she was ordained as a lay disciple of Shunryu Suzuki Roshi, the Zen master who helped spread Soto Zen Buddhism in the United States through his founding of the Tassajara Zen Mountain Center and San Francisco Zen Center, monasteries where Sher practiced for eleven years. In 1980 she left Zen

Center, having made the momentous decision to dedicate herself to writing, and shortly thereafter began publishing poems in little magazines in the Bay Area and elsewhere. Since then she has published forty-two books of poetry, three books on writing as a craft and a spiritual practice, and a book on bread making based on her years of experience at the San Francisco Zen Center's bakery in San Francisco. Following a degree in Clinical Psychology, she has been a practicing psychotherapist since 1990.

For readers who may be new to Sher's work, this collection offers both an introductory selection of her writing and, through her statements on poetics and biographical notes, some useful contexts for approaching it for the first time. For those who may already be familiar with Sher's individual publications and/or her appearances in magazines and anthologies, it provides the poet's own narrative of her development as a writer, beginning with her radical language experiments of the 1980s and 90s and continuing through her Asian influenced work (2000–2008), the wisdom mind collection (2008–2013), late work (2014–2018), and most recently new poems. These categories first appeared in Sher's *Reading Gail Sher* (2016), a collection of self-reflections and other resources mapping the evolution of her writing. While they indicate certain trajectories and patterns across the four decades of Sher's work, they do so only retrospectively. For the poet, every poem and every book begins as a new adventure, especially for a writer like Sher who believes that one should never write what one already knows and that, instead, the meaning(s) of a poem emerge(s) only during the experimental activity of writing it. To write, then, is to read, just as to read Sher's work is to take part in the action of writing (constructing) it, a process that she describes in "The *Way* of the Poem" as "co-creative."

Sher has stated that the books of her wisdom mind period are for her the culmination of her work as a writer in that they have been the most successful in terms of making possible certain kinds of attention for the reader. (Not coincidentally, while the other periods of her writing life are all represented with selections and in some cases excerpted texts, with some publications omitted, every title from the wisdom mind collection appears here in its entirety.) In the introduction to that section, she writes: "Between 2008 and 2013 I wrote a series of eight books ... that are rooted in Tibetan Buddhist philosophy and dedicated to 'stretching' English in order to create gaps so that Wisdom Mind might flow through to the reader....As a poet, I feel that this body of work is my most important."

What is this wisdom to which the poem aspires? Drawing upon Buddhist and other Eastern notions of awareness, it is an experience beyond the limits of the self that includes overlapping linguistic, spiritual, psychological, and ecological dimensions—a non-conceptual mode of thinking that is only knowable from inside the performance of the poem. To access this state of perception, Sher follows language beyond its semantic qualities so that the poet/reader may discover what else is possible when our habitual activity of sense-making is interrupted. For the poet, the challenge becomes how to inhabit the "tension" that is always present sonically in the word "attention," which here finds its source in the ongoing play and deferral of meaning in Sher's writing. Whether working with sequences of individual words in much of her early writing or later on with larger patterns of narrative coherence, her writing delights in the process of circling around but never settling into any determinate or conventional meaning. Instead, she offers us the gift of "using words to go beyond words."

For Gail Sher, writing is a necessary practice and discipline—a way of orienting one's mind and body in the word and in the world—in order to experience the intervals and silences in which other forms of mindfulness are present. In celebration of her longstanding commitment to poetry, the Poetry Collection is pleased to co-sponsor this publication of her *Poetry & Poetics, 1980–2020* by Night Crane, the press she founded in 1997 with her husband Brendan Collins. We hope this book—along with the resources of the Poetry Collection's Gail Sher Collection and Gail Sher Digital Collection—will help pass along her significant body of work and its many forms of attention to new generations of readers for many years to come.

JAMES MAYNARD
Curator, The Poetry Collection, University at Buffalo

## *Poetry, Zen and the Linguistic Unconscious*

As a girl I studied piano with a teacher whose idea of "playing with weight" intrigued me. I became aware not only of the heaviness or lightness of my stroke but to sounds (and overtones of sounds) thereby subtly modulated. Delicate gradations became a focus of control. Today, as a poet, it is not much of a stretch for me (regarding words) to be primarily concerned with their relative weight within, and as, a charged environment.

In college I studied music, literature and linguistics. I won a Ford Foundation Fellowship to continue with linguistics, but found the subject too abstract. I craved immersion— plush Middle English—(*The Parliament of Fowls, Troilus and Creseide, Sir Gawain and the Green Knight*). Yes. Music of a different sort.

Later, I entered a Zen community. Music wasn't allowed. At first I experienced this as a deprivation. But as I settled in, I began to choose it. I followed the monastic schedule and didn't think overly much about accomplishing anything. The spirit of "just doing"—just going along without attaching to ideas of gain or progress—became the foundation for my future work with words.

Still later, I discovered I needed to write and that I needed to do this outside of the Zen community. To survive the tremendous anxiety of not knowing what I was doing, a spirit of "just doing" came in handy. I would have "writing periods" instead of zazen periods. My vow was to attend them. I couldn't attach to accomplishing anything because I had nothing in mind to accomplish. The absence of striving radically opened my mind and heart. Gradually this approach morphed into using language in such a way that it functioned not symbolically but synchronistically (as Jung would say). The new "meanings" my language carried (and concerns that it addressed) derived from what I called the linguistic unconscious.

### A Linguistic Understanding

Although Suzuki-roshi
told John Cage that he had
nothing to say about music
or art, Cage still felt Suzuki
had led him to see music
'not as a communication
from the artist to an
audience, but rather as an
activity of sounds in which
the artist found a way to let
the sounds be themselves.'

Linguistics is the science of language—the study of the nature and structure of human speech. What I have discovered by entirely receiving what arises during my writing periods is <u>that</u> part of language based in the collective human psyche. It is a universal aspect of language rooted in a substrata of experience that goes beyond the individual's personal life. I have found that if I tap into this quality of a word, then anyone who listens to my work with the same acuity will be able to "understand" it.

The understanding is not semantic. It is not aligned to the particular signification we somewhat automatically attach to words. I use a word stripped of its semantic implications in order to highlight its relationship to vast galaxies of expression often overlooked. Humans are so programmed to use words according to what they "mean" that when the slightest loophole for "meaning" emerges, the mind instantly lights on this and doesn't see what else is there is.

It is important to note that the kind of interaction with language to which I refer is not the same as free association (a psychoanalyst who attended a poetry reading of mine once praised me for my "free association"). Free association is one's personal string of responses to an idea or image—a manifestation of one's unique personality or pathology. Jung pointed out that we can free associate to anything, including this morning's news, but the associations will invariably lead us to our personal complex of emotional/psychological issues. Like Freud, Jung uses the term unconscious both to describe mental contents which are inaccessible to ordinary awareness and to demarcate a psychic space with its own character, laws and functions. Jung regarded the unconscious as a locus of psychological activity which differed from and was more objective than personal experience since it related directly to the instinctual bases of the human race. The personal unconscious (Freud's discovery) rests on the collective unconscious (Jung's discovery, though at the end of his life Jung preferred the term "objective psyche"—the psyche as it is—to "collective unconscious"). The ground from which my work arises and the means by which it communicates is what I call the "linguistic unconscious," and I think of it as a manifestation of the "objective psyche" Jung described.

### A Spiritual Understanding

Dom Bede Griffiths, an Oxford-educated, English Benedictine monk who founded a monastery/ashram in India in 1955, writes:

> . . . a Buddhist saying has
> it: 'We use words to go
> beyond words and reach the
> wordless essence.' Human
> language derives from the
> physical nature of man.
> 'It was the nerves and not
> the intellect which created
> speech.'
>
> The word Brahman is said
> to derive from the root

brh, which means to swell
or to grow. This seems to
have signified originally
the rising of the word
from the depths of the
unconscious, the growth
into consciousness.[1]

In their critical introduction to the *Poems of Wang Wei*,
Willis and Tony Barnstone say that the voices one hears
in this eighth-century Chinese poet are those one hears
in absolute silence. For Wang Wei, silence was both a
personal discipline and the issue of his poetry. Indeed, in
Wang Wei's poems there are three levels of silence. The
first is the descriptive silence of the outer world. This
quiet world is a precondition for the second silence that is
spiritual, the silence of the mind. Which mind, purged of
distractions, gives rise to the third silence, the silence of
deepest meditation. "When thought stops, words halt, and
we move through light toward absolute stillness."[2]

When words are filled with silence, our ordinary
understanding of what is needed to convey meaning
completely changes.

Some years ago I wrote a prose poem called "The Intimacy

---

[1] Bede Griffiths, *The Marriage of East and West* (Springfield, IL: Templegate, 1982) 62-63.
[2] Tony Barnstone & Willis Barnstone, trans., *Poems of Wang Wei* (Hanover, NH: University Press of New England, 1991) xliv.

of the Silence." My subject was saturated language and how the writer uses silence to fill her words.

She infuses them with her own kind of silence and this is what creates her "voice." Examples of saturated language from writers I admire are in italics:

*The Intimacy of the Silence*

To saturate is to satisfy fully
to load to capacity
to fill completely
with something that
permeates
an indistinct plentitude
which is empty.

To saturate language
a writer must
silence herself
so that the word
pure passivity of being
is.

*She stiffened a little*
*on the kerb*
*waiting for Durtnall's van*
*to pass.*[3]

Blanchot explains that

---

[3] Virginia Woolf, *Mrs. Dalloway.*

tone is not the writer's voice,
but the *intimacy of the silence*
she imposes upon the word.
*He was gazing earnestly*
*at the little boy.*[4]

The silence is still his.
He preserves himself
within the work.

*At night*
*she would doze off*
*with morphine*
*and my mother and Grandpa*
*each drank*
*in their separate rooms.*[5]

Silence is felt as concentration.
*There she was perched,*
*never seeing him,*
*waiting to cross*
*very upright.*[6]
Movement within something enclosed.
A small action
or detail
with elaborate internal activity.

---

[4] Lady Murasaki, *The Tale of Genji*
[5] Lucia Berlin, "Dr. H.A. Moynihan" from *Phantom Pain.*
[6] Virginia Woolf, *Mrs. Dalloway.*

Logic is tension
and tension is transparent.

*He threw coffee on the fires,*
*staining the plastic-soft floor*
*a deep cave brown.*[7]

Breakups in a contextual,
denotative or linguistic sense
do not affect
the stream of concentration
continuity
which pushes the skin of a word
so that
saturated
it will stand alone.

*Don't you notice*
*something rather different*
*about his eyes?*[8]

When silence is used to fill words, and the gaps between words, the ordinary understanding of what is needed to convey meaning entirely changes. Words stand alone. Sounds <u>are</u> (are allowed to be) themselves. Anything more weakens the message.

---

[7] Lucia Berlin, "Dr. H.A. Moynihan" from *Phantom Pain*.
[8] Lady Murasaki, *The Tale of Genji*

*A Psychological Understanding*

Heinz Kohut, an innovative psychoanalyst who came
to the United States from Vienna during the Second
World War, founded a new school within psychoanalysis
called Self Psychology. (Self Psychology attaches greater
significance to the effect of relationships upon our
development than the effect of so-called innate instincts
like sex and aggression—Freud's concerns). Kohut was
keenly aware that the work of a great artist reflects the
central psychological problems of his era. In the following
passage from *The Restoration of the Self*, Kohut directly
addresses the issue of fragmented language:

> . . . the emotional problems of
> modern man are shifting, and
> the great modern artists were
> the first to respond in depth to
> man's new emotional task. Just as
> it is the understimulated child,
> the insufficiently responded-to
> child, the daughter deprived
> of an idealizable mother, the
> son deprived of an idealizable
> father . . . so it is the crumbling,
> decomposing, fragmenting,
> enfeebled self of this child and,
> later, the fragile, vulnerable,
> empty self of the adult that the
> great artists of the day describe

. . . and that they try to heal.
The musician of disordered
sound, the poet of decomposed
language, the painter and
sculptor of the fragmented
visual and tactile world:
they all portray the breakup
of the self and through the
reassemblage and rearrangement
of the fragments, try to create
new structures that possess
wholeness . . . [9]

Kohut points out that while the art of Henry Moore, O'Neill, Picasso, Stravinsky, Pound, and Kafka would have been unintelligible even a hundred years ago, today, precisely <u>because</u> of their intricate and nonsymmetrical order, we admire them for articulating the quality of our suffering.

*An Ecological Understanding*

Art, beauty and craft have
always drawn on the self-
organizing 'wild' side of
language and mind.
　　　　　*—Gary Snyder*

---

[9] Heinz Kohut, *The Restoration of the Self* (New York: International Universities Press, 1977) 286.

Gary Snyder claims that the fundamental nature of language is wild because "wild" is a name for the way that phenomena continually actualize themselves. Our ability to tune into that wildness—with greater and greater accuracy rendering it alive by depicting it in our self-reflections—ironically bespeaks of that very measure of health and wholeness, the lack of which so deeply concerns us. Our ability to stay present with the chaos may in the end be our salvation.

Although it might seem interesting to delve further into a theoretical exploration of my poetry, it would actually be unhelpful. My work is rarely intellectually based. In fact my biggest responsibility to myself as a poet is to remain in the realm of the unknown. I don't write what I already know, therefore I don't write from an idea or concept or from any other analytical place.

My writing arises, and I am constantly surprised by it.

### Afterword

This essay is based on a talk I gave at the School of Management and Strategic Studies at the Western Behavioral Sciences Institute in La Jolla, California in 1989.

Though the school no longer exists, it made a pioneering attempt to introduce its unusual audience (business executives, military officers, research administrators and scholarship participants from the public sector) to innovative ways of thinking and knowing.

Although I was not able to articulate then what I might say now about how I work as a poet, much of what I said remains true of my practice and understanding today:

—the Zen spirit of "just doing" (not knowing).
—daily writing periods instead of formal zazen.
—receiving what arises from levels of awareness that go beyond the personal.
—using words stripped of their conventional, semantic understanding.
—allowing the underlying "sound matrix," the foundation of language, to manifest.
—using words to go beyond words.
—recognizing silence as both a personal discipline and the issue of poetry.
—saturating language with one's own silence.
—fragmented language as an articulation of our psychological and social suffering, and an impulse toward its healing.
—chaos in language as a reflection of the wildness of nature itself.

Today I would simply say that I create space by making room for the mind to go to levels of understanding that language itself can't get to. My words just barely don't make sense. That creates a gap, a pause, and in the space of "not understanding" a deeper realization can occur.

My biggest responsibility as a poet hasn't changed: it is still to remain in the silence of the unknown.

# The Way of the Poem[1]

When a poem of uncertain portent maintains its own isolation and integrity, like music, an independent language all its own will sing the place, inviting the reader.

For music can perhaps be thought of as pure-logic divested of the bothersome friction of words.

Along with the words we ingest the pure logic that is realized on its own, with its own wit, its own far-infrared dialectic.

A handful of parentheses sets a mood for the optional and that's all you have, like the flick of a conductor's wand.[2]

>           geshé geshé
>           you hook the word
>
>           o Usnisavijaya
>           (Shukden of despoil)
>
>           to gull the sky
>           sweet full of northwest flowers

---

[1] From *Reading Gail Sher*.
[2] Parentheses don't contain. They shield. As Kathleen Fraser points out, they are also "a usuage which women continue to find useful in breaking out of a misleading sense of stability." *Poetics Journal*, no. 4, May 1984, p. 100.

I am tall
I am slow full
walker [3]

*Memory*

A poem has its own memory.

And the poem's memory provides a *feeling* context to
the private memory of each word.

Their inter-change creates a field.

"I SEE it," says a reader who then sallies along smell-
ing all the flowers.

First seeing, then entering the poem's field, in part
authors the poem's memory.

Actually poetry is memory, endowing words with a
kind of eternity.

*Allure*

While the poet's oral rendering of her poem is a
powerful venue for the poem, sometimes *on the page* a
voice can be more "catchable."

Being drawn into its world, partaking of that world
such that for the moment of the poem, *you* are the
person, affected.

---

[3] *Who,* a Licchavi, p. 43.

Certain poems, like Paris, so completely BELIEVE in themselves that their world—even one word— becomes an entire creed.

> I see a photograph of her throat, which is not the actual throat. *Where is her throat in the wake of <u>that</u>?* (I'm guessing *that* means *after* her throat.)[4]

*Repetition*

From here, one adds the element of repetition. (I almost said "passion.")

When a word repeats it seems more genuinely to be one's feeling.

Repetition soothes and instills desire. "Tell me again," "read it again," like a record one will play over and over and over, digging the groove inside the soul that played it over and over even before it was born.

Counting, a "take-off"—da-t'-da, da-t'-da, da-t'-da, da-t'-da—it's in the human gene.

The "hook" of the word creates the safety-of-environment. We need to feel safe to risk slipping through a gap.

Poetry *is* dangerous, after all.

---

[4] *White Bird*, p. 68.

*Gaps*

The marrow of the style is gaps. Hiatus and lucid gaps.

Lurking behind would be a story verging on revealing itself were the gaps colored in.

The reader gets an invite—"Please, dear reader, color me in"—such that the poem is co-creative, the revelation is co-creative, shaping itself to each individual's paradigm.

> Mother's warm breath, like a *plate* of breath. Yet it is old breath, having eaten many crackers.
>
> *My breath is a wall*, she whispers from *real* breath, instantly present to birds.
>
> The energy of the animal appears to be experienced internally, its breath (a shadow) withheld in its own stem.
>
> What's left of mind as a squirrel leaps out?[5]

Pacing a poem by breaths not only creates an intensity but also a sense of ongoingness.

For what is language and what is breathing, the one propelling and originating the other?

---

[5] *Mother's Warm Breath*, p. 79.

The words elude while the breaths make a philosophy.

Syntax is the motion.

Each word has it own syntax,

*Searching Energy*

Each word has a location so that when we hear a word, unconsciously we expect for it.

Just naturally, by virtue of the human mind.

We complete what is happening by *listening* it. (We HEAR th*e* word into LIFE.)

The mind, activated by a word, allows its affective nature to touch it.

> Sparrows seem used, uninvented.
>
> Scaly mud, dull sky, colorless birds, remind me of my mind.
>
> To see the autumn leaves scatter in my home. (The longing they arouse as they lie on the wood turning red.)
>
> Is it of my body that they partake?[6]

---

[6] *Watching Slow Flowers*, p. 58.

*Searching Energy + Stumping Mind*

Using words to baffle the mind releases the brilliance of the mind.

The language breaks. The mind is stopped.

When, barring understanding, words must instead be grasped—

> thru Him marigold
> summertime
> summertime
>     bluefish
>     (pokeweed)
>         WANTED
>     kept cups[7]

we hear the silence objectified.

*Weight*

"Weight"—not of the poem (the *matter* of the poem) but the "hand" of the poet as she writes.

Like a pianist, a poet can bear down, but her bearing down is internal.

For language is an instrument that bears weight, dare one say, even more sensitively.

---

[7] *Marginalia*, p. 94.

Not is good also. Not is a mechanism, like
picking on a banjo, that to weight, by its nature, is
impervious.

> *China bloodless boy*

> people of mast
> here are some

> if we are dumb
> if we are dumb

> so puffed and
> slobbering to themselves

> \*

> shouting it
> down the mountain

> lugging the beast
> back to his people

> \*

> over hills, over fields
> the moon's condition
> come to pass

> *come home stars*
> *lay down your heads*

nailed to the earth
across the pasture[8]

*Rhythm: the internal rhythm of a word and the overall river
of words*

Rhythm is the bedrock, the voice, the fundamental
principle upon which a poem is built.

Rhythm *is* the "what" of what's being said because
"how" is what's being said.

A continuous flow, for example, suggests that
thoughts themselves are contiguous though not
exactly *causing* one another.

Rhythm keeps the music clean. It *spells* the pulse of
cyclical existence.

> *tiger tiger*
> from Yarlung Valley head
>
> arising from the flower
> from the bath
> of ancient wood
>
> Tara of the neck
> help me through
> this birth

---

[8] *Calliope*, p. 14.

draw the word
through its beauteous
hole[9]

*Linkage*

*Renga* (Japanese) are linked poems of varying length launched by a *haiku*.

Often composed in a group setting, each poet jams off the previous poet's offering, grounding by links what otherwise might seem lame.[10]

The best links are invisible. They register, but on a first hit, not as a thought, but a flow.

Though *renga* are associated with *haiku*, the strategy, linkage, works just as well in other settings. (Note the current page and the one previous.)

*Saturation*

To saturate means to fill—to flood, glut, overload. To imbue or suffuse, to impregnate, permeate, steep.

Each word carries its absolute full load *so that* there is little distraction or waste of time (leakage).

The poet stuffs each word into a little canon. It socks the reader.

---

[9] *Who* a Licchavi, p. 27.
[10] For an example, see: Gail Sher and Andrew Schelling, "Hundred-Stanza Renga," *Simply Haiku*, vol. 8, no. 2, Autumn 2010.

RADICAL LANGUAGE EXPERIMENTS, 1980-1997

## *Introduction*

When I first began writing, everything was a test. I had
no idea of writing "poetry." I never read poetry. I avidly
read prose. But my concerns, as I reluctantly learned, were
all of them of a poet, not a novelist, short story writer or
essayist. I came to understand that I am a poet because I
think like a poet. And it was singularly poets and poet-
editors who first saw and supported my work. An early
underlying feature—that my writing simply arose—
remains to this day. I don't write what I already know,
or perhaps, stated more exactly, since my writing stems
primarily from the "linguistic unconscious" and not from
everyday consciousness, I find it a continual surprise.

## She stood all divine in her lash.

Grand her very presence look voice the mere contemporaneous fact of whom multiplied by sudden magical amounts the accuracy with which he heard what he had said just as she had heard it. Various. Fifty women. Her young eyes bred like linen for a wedding the effort of an age awaiting that ceremony. They unwrapped him.

*The infelicity and confusion of his arm now bent around her eagerness.*

Like a bride and always about her the breath almost of happy wonderful special. All this about-to-be wait-and-see she wore in her blonde hair and the lilt with which she tip-chinned shook it back behind her an asset the measure of her wealth taken thereby by what she took so displayingly for granted. Her pretty perfect teeth her very small too small nose deferring with count-onable ease a deference he most assuredly counted on counted more than he could say on its ready assignation. This quantity the crease of his lambswool jacket confident and loose hang of tie collected so completely that her tea-table vitality pleasant public familiar served and radiantly settled over him an altogether different an altogether self affirmation.

*He fancied them liked them and passing through them with her more slowly now.*

Her room was high and cool and bare and opened on another room bare to fullness with sun. Here leaning gently pressing her cheek against the side of the recess she saw flowers a miracle of cheapness an exposure kept in durance as an approach her primary furniture to what she can have thought a full and formal air. Producible. Amazing.

Excerpt from: *Credences: A Journal of Twentieth Century Poetry & Poetics*, Vol. 1, No. 1. Buffalo: The Poetry Collection, University at Buffalo, 1981. The final version of the complete poem is in Gail Sher, *Early Work*. See bibliography for details.

*She stood all divine in her lash.*

## From another point of view
### the woman seems to be resting

Naive or feelings of isolation
and at the same time naive.

The same woman only a feeling
of sun now arrested on the floor
near her chair. Rocking and
making various gestures in
concentrated posture.

From another point of view the
woman seems to be resting.
Perhaps this resting is what brings
the fields into play. Figures appear.
The sky and the woman each
unsurrounded. The sound (of no
concern to anyone else)
into which she feels drawn suddenly

This scene gives the impression
of fields. Separated from fields
by a porch.

Settles in watchful
gesture.

Gradual ability. Settles
in place for reading and
life of reading as

insisted internal thing.

Speaks about it softly.
Volition as a kind of
thought. Attributes of
body (sun) and muscles
of body. (Also light in
marked relationship.)

Somewhat confused sense or
some boastfulness coupled
with something else.

Time and also clouds.
Texture of clouds
and so forth in a
continuous line or
pattern.

Landscape and trees.
(Haze of trees.)
Shoulders arms or
occasional repetitive
thought.

Now reads. Imagines
herself in the dark
room.

Something recognized
as dark. Shouts for
the little girl.

Presses forward to
some extent.

Moments held clean and intact
now appears as a wall. (Method
and exposure to first thought.)

The expression fixed.
Points of softness
absolutely seen by
someone else.

Seeing heavily or seeing
effects of known sedentary
person. (Inclusive of her
in an early period.)

Provides a certain luminosity
of detail. At the same time
balance.

Suggestions in this vein.
(Objects) existing in
unheard sound. (Both color)
and the boundaries of all
objects hitherto mentioned.

Trees but basically the
house is the same.

Reads with attention on
trees shifts entering into

balanced reading.

Or woman lying reading.
Paraphernalia of mind seen
as objects coming to a
complete rest.

*Also as a child she had wanted to eat*

Also as a child she had
wanted to eat.

Without particular motive
(to be) on her own crossing
the street on her own or
going through the door
making an effort to buy
food.

Always with amount of energy
she could spend with that
person (son) or even possibly
some other people.

Even simply listening. Not
urged to but that that had
 already occurred.

Seen by the other people
(during) the day or sometime
during the course of the

day (the driver) calls out something.

To be phased by this. To
appear calm but actually
to imagine herself
quarreling.

Intense expression in
striving for something
(intake) of food
(inheritance) of
something.

Having asked for something
to eat (in) one process
to eat one (particular)
part.

In bed for example (always)
perpetuating (striving) in
the midst of any room.

Which (she) as a lonely
person appreciated.

Avenues and walking with
such & such emotion (buses)
where they seem needed.

Reversing her terminology
and tendency to want
something from him. (To)

supply food here. (Not)
to move or feel like moving.

With others like her
in the same mood (hiding)
something received from
her.

Delicate relation to her
(discerned) (quarter) of
mind.

Children & events of the
day enter her mind. Once
while eating (in) quiet
manner of saying something.

Or being in a hurry to get
somewhere. Arrangement of
food at (moment) of giving
it to her.

*Even the lady's pressure next to her*

Powerful inner lapse or
undivulged sense. (Also)
him in the capacity of
boy.

Pictures of him. Related
in way of terrific scene
(bed) or warm with hand in
book of him.

Through caring charged tone.
Age & body as well as
also this caring.

Days later in place of
children (to) see in others
the possibility of her
body.

Receptive position requiring
this blessing. Short breaths
of sun (minerals) in lap of
her.

Always eats (sings) walks
near river humming & singing.

Focused on point of
milling crowd (assembly)
of persons (windows) doors

& many people in them
looking away.

(Conversation) of woman
in curious posture.

(One) face (eventual)
eloquence of her.

Which moves in her. This
abstraction (which) this
pain was.

Even the lady's pressure
next to her.

(Roughness) of feet also
some cleaning of the room.

Slender girl or (old)
purpose of united her.

With spread of her (sings)
probing also words.

Waits for bus. Borrows man's
capacity (what) lay behind
in pastime of several minutes.

Quantities of people among
them (visualized) poised
person (alert) posture of
gratitude.

Or in towards her. To utter
it (to) please refurbish
life compelling in this
respect.

Kneels before him (how) he
felt alone. Fragrance of
wood (nails) appealing to
her.

Travels in sphere of white
or unhappy face. (Ignites)
death response (her) in
group of waking men.

Defining it (or) reads about
rapture to break this
pattern.

To be awake like this if
not disappointment to be
aware of them redeeming
themselves.

*Perhaps there is no content paint or sun*

Perhaps there is no content
paint or sun. Wood or light.
1) Makes loving motion as of
kissed one 2) Achieves
resistance on a black surface.

Private inner weight. Conceives
reality of strokes placed on the
paper carefully. Somewhat
revised circumstance (temper) of
hand.

(Will) mesh in with only
one passively assembled
tone. 1) Elements of brown
(tree) (justifiable) pitch
2) As a novelty or given
content in the dress of a
woman.

Concentrates on pattern with
(repetitious) conception of
her eating.

Conception of her addressing
someone. Percentage of words
(inward breathed words) along
these lines.

Joined by points though

propelled in free-floating
something (which is) how
color works.

As within sleep something
including him sleeping in
the other room. Also the
woman on the bed. Easily
takes suggestion from the
girl writing. 1) Whether
from frightening circumstance
2) Short pause imposed from
without 3) Repeats this
constantly.

Completes act of eating
(alone) tired & depressed
before eating. 1) Only
certain portions of this
2) This and religion
(certain) rosaries.

A wedge or sound no one
notices. Like a lot of
red (in restful building)
or drives up very
solemn.

Which turns into eating
or ability of someone
with talent.

## (As) on things which (headpiece) touches the Moslem

(As) on things which
(headpiece) touches
the Moslem

In who claim
to hold
(to) be
form ( dearest)

Or even some grabbing
to brace
(to) be
sectional protecting
jacket

Saw (too) to
cling here
chessmen

Red air chews
yes

This queer
bare
mouth

Ignites the mother
beak

Or man on the dais
as its mother
stroked it

Mime is first

Part mint part
internal march
quantity

No guy

Nor flaps of
voice to part
this

So tentacles or
them

Retreat itself

Chant wrought
side

Is lewd or solicits
lewd

The grit or
hear

Which comes
student

Vows & pick

*(As) on things which (headpiece) touches the Moslem*   37

here

Whereas derives
stallion inside

Exact were
larvae
also

Eat line
green on
love

The jut will
hoarse Christ
eventually

Renunciant line
excepts

A dent from
month

Hand & mung
born dark

Dram nun

To opens in a
lower room

Brittleness high
love

Bring the pull
strains graced
which vesicle

Like hills leave
to various hills

This time the
clasp food

Or anniversary of a polite
act

Being a toy building
from one kiln

Hex these
lake

The crock the
shepherd on
her own children
thankfully

The woolly flesh

Or part which
stampedes even music
basically

And elegance its
tenancy

Doer logs ferrying
cells

A rung or
yelling underneath
the honey

Tensile lowing
most young

Joins others I
the unguent
I

Tubers & iron
even to prepare
this

This elliptical
weaning or long
spaying sound

Wheels all right
this dark math
earth

Or widow's phone

As hover from the
elbows is something
growing

Bittenness as

monk

Pat on
this

Taking one
ignite

Girl and no

Bond to gum

Intense from
now

The hoist pin

Dawns or
parson

Or go god

To swill
could

These pear and
sand year

Must sipping
thinks

Opaque strains
together to
clap

Tries august

Calf the inch

Lady wife
they fallen
birds

Crayons geese
its unkind
horse

This alert
dots

*(As) on things which (headpiece) touches the Moslem*

## Rouge to beak having me

Rouge to beak
having me

Banner this
could be

During wane
were along
river

Tribes or limb

Swabs metal
cattle

Styes scanned

Were considers
total
colony

Sachels north spines
still

Adorable can

That beads so
death

Rushes Yule say

family

These sprig
hare can
scrapings
father

Whether ark
girdles deer

Graining said

Constant would
munch its
body

Low bud
deers

Chews cry
momentarily deers

Sets which
elephant

Receives said
having
rotation

II.

Spill to whose
one

Be gasped mine
drum samples

Dry straps:
no pureness

No woo is

Sole kinder

What knob
selves

Whew (or)
mass

Dimmer &
biers math

No scour
fur

Mongers is
stilling

Or find
accumulations

(Bundt) lift
to prize
one

Ones skim
faultless

Mollusk foams
so twist
himself

Grace (still)
fruit

Geer: pike
to fruit

Budges of:
auks (why)
shyster

Fond out

Maws as
tone

Wings licks
as

Tryst yet: dual

Trees (the)
kite
tithe

Freezes stud (to)
garnish
thee

Behests peering

candies

Twins (particles)
aunt
so

Fey (to)
band

Wombs: ham
(so) told
dirigible

III.

Exemplifies sags
(ma) I do

Bowls cattle
sacred girl

If cereal
were blueish
nights

Purges (bowl)
(gloves) ugliness
for her

Peas one abdomen

Piquant constructs
(heals) what

queue

Bleeds proms
is (in)
soul

Briars ol' bud

Petals food
(stripling) whose
disciples graze
could

Sluts wept
arm

Gunny names

Nibs prayer
melodically

Law snows (corn)
as poverties
at her

Beads words:
reeds etched
yet

Prolapsed heard (bull)
stuffs

Plentiful skins

men sounds

Does mounds:
(annuity) feels
gowns on

(Flies) either
singer

Stringent folds:
throngs will

Abound: abounds
his

Drinks afresh:
studs neuter (moist)
count

Micro (winters)
further

Swallow has
shrill (some)
terribly
dawn

Peters (the) self
jails undress

The flee:
(either) sides
pulse

# KUKLOS[1]

Tamrind Esau.

& taps.

Kadish.

Clam St. Clare
    too faces.

Jasper roach

cans Mishna
    redwing.

Betel has like
    dipso trough.

Padma so bath.

Criss par
    trinity.

Hath Da.

Peanut Hosanna.

Wassail pied
    cum

---

[1]KUKLOS (Greek): circle, circular body; circular motion, ring, wheel, disc, eye, shield; town wall.

brindle ergo.

Horse o' sphinx.

America. Non
    dalmatian.

*

Turbo fra.

Islet rebec
    daybed.

I manna
    cossack.

Bodhgaya. Soeur
    roe Padua.

Milagro. Cunt
    un.

Baptist ash.

Meaty noh
    poi.

Kurmos. New
    gorse.

Pony sweetyard.

Contessa bushes.

Too feces. Gazetier.

Angst 'cause
    paison.

Tilsit. Lacre
    tarpaulin.

Saguaro letterer.

Pistol catalpa.
Their shells.

\*

Skater skater.

Eighty cantina
    maypole.

Pachinka capa moor.

Yenta. Ne'er
    galina.

Kapok roses.

Tailor tailor. Mimosa
    a mitt.

Charybdis in
    queen.

Scyla. Swaha.

Mahjung. Schnaps.

Bris of

Odessa rice laps.

*

Grazes Mu
corona.

Pied carrot.

Telos Balaam
nicolo.

O-chai fete.

Compline flushing

raga hey
seeds.

Hibiscus. Non seraph.

Spinaker.
Agnus
thru sayeth.

Eros Dei caritas.

Oxlips Gaias
ga-te ga-te.

Helix @ lane.

Sannyas crow Janaki.

Loden cloth.
Bonny Dom catched.

\*

Osiris co rider.

Hanuman cup.
Cam floatation
shiksa.

Okasa askari.

Ganjha blouse
Goth sydeco
salaam.

Piper fra
Galilee.

Ashkenazi traps.

Well furze.
Tapes pique
    trumpeter.

Goby gnu
assize.

Lo cod.

Sabine the reichstag.

Tivoli wight.

The atone sri.

Joseph angus
    lassitude.

*

Savannah mejda.

Flocks.

Nu madonna
sahib.

Leechee simcha.
Taj mesquite
pease.

Witch Mt. kyke.

Bracken mate.
O' entire madden.

Infested rouges
shabrack.

Yangtze Gretal. Corazon.

Salon ex davin.

Rivka Shaker they've
    sorti.

Kachina fire.
Sunyata bambino
in names.

Gelt. Fellatio
tempest doña.

Nicholas. Wotan
garment.

*

To drumline geese.

Satyr Gobi. Niños
   Carolina.

Tunny mullet Bowbells.

Kennedya jibon.
Jheel roy
vulpine persea.

Padma frumenty.

Lhasa to bade.

Tulip Dachau.
This Alps.

Negrillo.

Shaman asana
fell

jai.

Sol du lavash.

Esdras. Hum.

Baruch. Rune.
Tamadua.

Cant Perpetua.

Laid.

The Gretal ta-ke.

ASIAN-INFLUENCED WORK 2000-2008

## *Introduction*

Taking writing as a practice followed eleven years of Zen
training. Living a monastic life with its strict schedule
of zazen (sitting meditation), assigned work, *dharma*
talks, *dokusan* (interviews with one's teacher), and the
concentrated reading of Zen texts immersed my mind
and body in an ancient Japanese culture. In addition to
Japan, my Asian-influenced poetry derives from India,
China, and Tibet and draws from Zen, Tibetan Buddhism
and the yoga traditions of India, all of which I studied
and practiced for many years after leaving the zendo.
The autobiographical writing of *The Moon of the Swaying
Buds* was written in the spirit of Japanese *haibun* (prose +
*haiku*); *Look at that Dog All Dressed Out in Plum Blossoms*
was influenced by the four-line Chinese *kanshi;* the
foundation for *RAGA* was the Indian raga and for *DOHĀ*
the Tibetan devotional song.

from
## The Moon of the Swaying Buds

### BOOK ONE: MOUNTAINS

There has always been a slight feeling of discomfort, a
lack of gracefulness in my relationship with activities.
During long summer afternoons, I'll lie on a cot on our
upstairs porch feeling astray, a foreigner to the porch.
Or I'll wander up the block to a field where I catch
butterflies. There are monarchs and swallowtails as well as
grasshoppers and other interesting bugs. I doze in the sun
and capture one or two. The idea of catching butterflies
sparks my imagination. I think, "I'll go across the street
and catch butterflies," and then, while I do, I think, "It's
a beautiful sunny day and I am catching butterflies." But
there is a gap. I am disrupted in myself and cannot enter
the activity, offer it enough of myself to make it come alive.


*up*
*down*
*tiny canyon butterfly*

Our dining room is covered with thick black wallpaper.
Embedded in its blackness are turquoise and pink birds.
Since family rarely go there (it is saved for company), it
acquires a mysterious largeness—like an empty chapel—
where I love to stand and stare out the window.

*empty now*
*my parakeet's cage*
*rattles in the wind*

I like to bake cookies. I like to read in my green chair and be under the covers writing in my diary. I like to knit. These activities involve my hands. I have a lot of "hand energy" that must be expressed or I feel at loose ends.

*sudden squall—*
*I wrap my hands*
*around the teacup*

I read *Seventeen* and imagine myself in control of my life, which to me means having a consistent and likable self-image. "I have a cocoa brown skirt, soft-colored sweaters, and oxford shoes and that is what I wear." Or "I have one or two navy blue skirts and many white blouses and that's all." Each plan appeals to me as a means of consolidation. As I stare at the girls in *Seventeen* and read the advice in its articles, I hang onto the words as if everything depends on getting this correct.

*so insistent—*
*the buzz of the fly*
*trapped in the unplugged fridge*

Nancy Drew's loner spirit mirrors my own yet-unformed one. Tracking herself assiduously from the perspective of the clues in her current "mystery," she uncovers a deeper level of reality. When I recognize in George Eliot the same ability to implode the specific with the infinite, it dawns on me (not as a thought but as an impulse) to live my life this way.

*instar:*
*ever-so-slowly*
*through the tangled foliage*

I like the pause of breakfast and certain fragments of my walk to school—a particular patch of sweet fresh air or a house set back from the street in an intriguing way. And of course Christ the King with its exotic parochial climate. I like the fact that there are bells at school, that time is clearly delineated, though the bells themselves are harsh, not subtly eliciting cosmic overtones like the Zen bells in my later life that deeply stir one's primal lethargy.

*night jasmine:*
*lighting my path*
*your white blossoms*

I subscribe to the magazine *The Writer*, the action in itself carrying a certain unfamiliar yet tingly sort of professionalism. But when *The Writer* arrives it feels off, wooden and impersonal. The tingly wool of my coverlet, the pregnancy of my guppy, the coziness of my green chair all seem oceans apart from "News," "Deadlines," and "Classifieds"

> *thunderheads occlude the sky*
> *at dawn, at dusk . . .*
> *the moon's absent face*

The fateful words of my father, "Oh, everyone wants to be a writer at one time or another" insert themselves in my being like a violation. My budding "identity" collapses in the face of his savvy. Of course. I should have known. The wish to be a writer is plebeian, trivial, predictable. Everyone wants to be *that*.

*raising it*
*shaking it*
*then tucking it*
*in its*
*breast*

BOOK FOUR: SKY

Rain warms the mountain air and feels soothing as it softly falls through the moonlight. Shallow drafts brush my face. Whereas minutes ago I felt reluctant, tired, mean, suddenly I am overcome with gratitude. In the *zendo* I sit bolt upright, supported by the gurgling creek. A chorus of birds are so ardently chirping that there seems to be a wall of raspy but sweet wet life surrounding me on all sides.

> *drizzly day . . .*
> *darts and wiggles*
> *in the waterweed*

Morning *zazen* ends. We leave our cushions and the primordial quiet that sinks in with the raindrops. The steady pound of rain, its persistent motion, makes our straight-backed cross-legged posture seem all the more still. By the end of second period we are nestled here forever.

*a train whistle blows . . .*
*perched in a tree*
*crow closes its eyes*

Tassajara is about breathing, and by extension, the next
level of care necessary for the body so that it can breathe—
an allotted amount of sleep, three balanced meals, a bath,
a period of study and rest from work every fifth day.
Much attention is lavished on all aspects of these activities
so that washing one's clothes takes its rightful place as
a primary concern. One needs clothes for breathing.
Therefore one must be prepared to sew or buy them,
mend them, wash them, store them so that they stay clean
and available.

*fog rolls in*
*fat gulls*
*huddle over the water*

Chop chop chop. The carrot is now a row of paper-thin, salad-ready (they are too skinny for soup or mixed vegetables) slices. I am momentarily in control. Chopping block, *hocho* (knife) and me standing, cutting the decisive widths. I feel exhausted, but the wafer-size carrot wheels are perfect.

> *Bashō*
> *your rainproof paper hat*
> *made with your own hands*
> *the one imitating Saigyō's . . .*
> *I too have felt desperately alone*

At Tassajara it rains. I have told the *tenken* I am sick and to please bring me hot water in a thermos, later, after breakfast. From my bed I hear the rain softly falling and the sound lulls me back to sleep. A band of moonlight criss-crosses my otherwise darkened cabin.

> *cooling the night with its plashing*
> *I doze . . .*
> *dream of its plashing*

Sometimes the wake-up bell will ring, with its primitive and unmistakably firm ring, and I cannot get out of bed. I lay there in the dark, in the glorious warmth of my sleeping bag, feeling remote, reluctant to decide to be at this monastery. The desire to stay in bed, finally to sleep enough, to be warm, to reconsider my life is overwhelming.

*hatched*
*but slow to uncoil*
*in the mild rain*

Through this "sickness" my life emerges. First I "get" that I am sick, the vast extent of it. Then I recognize the tremendous energy that I bestow on the things I choose to do. I can't help but ask why I pour myself into sewing, for example, and sneak out of *zazen,* when it is *zazen* I have presumably come to Tassajara to practice.

> *full moon—facing it*
> *knees braced*
> *beneath my robe*

The answer is evident in my hands. My hands write and sew with immaculate, single-minded passion, passion that is sure of itself, pulsating and ecstatic. In the *zendo* my hands freeze. All the contraptions I can devise to insulate them beneath my robes cannot prevent their stiffening numbness.

*winds howl*
*snow mounts*
*the wintry thicket . . . lifeless*

One holds out for so long then gives oneself over to a chain of events by which isolated segments of one's life unravel. The contents scramble. The life force, renewed, released, slowly reconstructs itself, as if one's karma metastasizes.

*autumn leaves*
*lie quietly*
*in the sun*

One day I have the following thought: "I have spent eleven years as a Zen student resisting everything. What would happen if I take all the energy that I put into resisting and use it for something positive?"

*eaglet*
*ripping the soldier*
*free from the asphalt*

From this seed I develop "yes practice." "Yes practice" means doing only those things that I say "yes" to with my whole body and mind. I will not get out of bed until there is something I want that much. (I have to find out if there is.) If there isn't, I will just die, but I am not going to pretend for another second.

*shrouded in fog*
*a tiny dinosaur*
*inches toward dawn*

Soon it occurs to me that I want to write. Whereas formerly I felt I needed a specified subject, now I think: "If I want to write, I'm going to write. I'm going to write a certain number of hours a day just like I go to *zazen* a certain number of hours a day. I will not worry about what I write. I will concern myself solely with attending my writing periods."

*high noon*
*lime-green sulphurs*
*mud-puddle in the canyon dust*

I am through with Zen Center. I need to define my own regime. Zen Center has had it with me anyway. I am told privately that unless my attitude changes, I will not be accepted for Fall Practice Period. Indeed, my attitude has changed but not in the direction that would pique my interest in Fall Practice Period.

*after the storm*
*over the hill . . .*
*zigzagging*

Saying "yes" finally was like a birth. And, like most other births, it came after a long period of gestation characterized by saying "no" only the "no" was unconscious. Immersed in the fog of my unconscious "no," I failed to recognize my own authenticity.

*tadpoles!*
*bug-eyed and squirmy*
*in their bracken-shaded mud*

A predominant feature of this inauthenticity was a sense of impending doom. Initially it hovered around the dreaded unnamed seemingly unavoidable crisis one could feel swelling in my childhood household. The atmosphere of this swelling—forces at work that I didn't understand, the largeness of those forces (that they were way, way beyond me), my ensuing inertia and blankness, and the resulting compliance (compliance being a form of inertia)—infiltrated all my subsequent endeavors, until "yes practice" broke through the gridlock.

*warming earth—*
*its scent*
*in an early-spring breeze*

Likewise in college, my inability to think and to write perpetuated the sense of being stalked—that at any moment something cataclysmic might happen. Because I couldn't keep up.

*a*
*falcon*
*circles*
*evermore*
*narrowly*
*down*
*through*
*the*
*desolate*
*sky*

Determining to say "yes" . . . making that a conscious act—housing the bits of emptiness and despair that belonged to me and then offering them to the universe— "Yes practice" meant claiming my life. "Yes practice" was the beginning of living my life as opposed to an ersatz life.

*waving long legs*
*dragging itself through the widening split*
*in the pre-dawn light*

Buddhism, also an attempt to heal the unpindownable sense of vacuousness that pervaded my life, turned out to be another trap. I began sitting *zazen* because I had come to the end of the way of life to which my parents had brought me up. I needed a deeper path—to access a larger part of myself. I didn't know what this meant exactly. It wasn't formulated mentally. I was drawn to *zazen* however at an important turning point.

*from broken shell*
*to clump of bluestem . . .*
*making a dash for it*

I tried very hard to follow the schedule because I believed that I had finally found—consummate and unfathomable—a path that plumbed the core of my being. Despite the fact that it was difficult, I told myself that at least I was on the right track. If I could just exert a little more effort, a little more will, a little more self-discipline . . .

*flat pink sea:*
*saffron wings*
*flutter over the prawn boat*

Ironically, the vehemence behind my determination hooked me irretrievably into another tailspin (I can't do it and there's no other choice). As I focused my energies on adjusting to the community (this, I was assured over and over, is Zen practice—"Just follow the schedule," everyone said, "while you notice mentally the obstacles that arise for you"), I failed to notice my unmitigated sense of hollowness and despair.

*slipping on the scree*
*her wings smeared*
*my fingers powdery*

The milieu of "yes practice" is movement. It includes ever-changing me. Doing only those things that I say "yes" to with my whole body and mind releases me minute by minute to become who I am.

*from the prow of the ferry*
*watching them spin ever faster*
*over the bay*

After I formally left Zen Center, I moved into a neighborhood apartment and for awhile continued to sit *zazen*. One day I had an interview with the Head Monk. He asked about my leave-taking and I carefully explained "yes practice." He said to me: "Until you say yes, you cannot practice Buddhism."

*an arctic basks—*
*wings tilted toward*
*the salmon pink sky*

from
*Look at That Dog All Dressed Out in Plum Blossoms*

*Snail breeze on a shaft of moon*

A dawn moon awakens me, softly softly, its waning light.

Dew sparkles on the cobweb-veiled grass.

Still in my nightgown, I carry my dream to the blue porch rail.

Neither dew nor dewy cobwebs dull the song of birds.

*"Let's go, babe!" says my dad a snapshot later*

Pale rain – daisies drink you sumptuously.

Sun peaks out behind your silky curtain of beads.

I wander through my garden, crocus and trillium asleep.

Have you stopped? No. Yes. For a moment I thought so.

*Asleep but easily startled*

Fishing along the quiet, unfrequented banks of the river.

Cryptomeria grove dark, even as late as noon.

A sudden rain, a breeze. A butterfly investigates my lunch. "Hello!"

Like the poet I wonder, "How long will lovely days like these last?"

*"The sudden moon alarms mountain birds"*

After diving into red lotuses, a cormorant soars over clear water.

Feathers sleek, fish in beak, it stands erect on an old drifting log.

Poet, you describe the water bird with such accuracy and passion,

yet isn't it the log you have come to feel is yourself?

*In numinous light the river raptly tranquil*

My small room has an eastern exposure. Cool in summer.
   Warm at dawn.

A pair of lovebirds purrs iridescence throughout the long
   quiet night.

Creamy roses, richly fragrant, merge their scent with the
   throbbing mist.

A friend cut some and presented them to me in a vase.


*Back from fishing*

Acrid yet fresh. Life fresh. (That certain not-yet putrid.)

Boat, body, bay, all dressed in it.

Can I wash it off? Herons can't.

The sea's insignia, in blood till death.

*Wild rose, wilder with the glow worm*

At a suq, was it you I thought I recognized?

Not the meat, the fruit, nor fattened greens.

Your fleeting face, or was it mine, behind a gauzy curtain,

the bazaar deserted, it being after dark and about to close.


*I didn't realize it was raining*

I ashore, you adrift. What are we doing?

My gaze follows you, placidly.

We've parted before. The stages of sorrow I've memorized.

The expanse of blue waves is impossible to fathom,
    lifetimes later.

*What happened to the moon in the enamored
monk's moonlit waters?*

Red fish in the ice-cold lake (crystal clear yet crinkled like
    a shoe).

A sand bar gleams beneath threatening clouds.

I lie on my back watching them unravel the northern hill.

Your voice, when you courted me, comes to mind.


*Frogs, the birds of night*

Snuggling in ("for the long haul" it feels) or at least the
    thought is delightful.

I tug the sheet around my ears, sink my body into its
    shroud.

Wind sweeps through the garden, a relief, will the heat
    break?

I am still. Absolutely and entirely one-pointed in stillness.

*"The dark moss already bears my print"*

One jay caws.

The forest and my heart resound with memory.

Not of jays, but of myself, not yet ready.

Not yet not.


*White lily in her devil's needle cloak*

Young shoots through an old fence.

That's me, the fence, trying to keep people away.

I tell them I'm celibate. I say I'm a monk.

Raindrops, dewdrops, the sodden leaves outside my gate.

*Peach-size in a peach field*

With ordinary monks I have nothing in common.

Spines straight, legs crossed, sitting-robes fraying at the
knees.

Drowsy in the morning, I watch for awhile, yawn.

Chores finished for the night, I brush my teeth and go to
bed.




*At town's end, the creaking flight of a grasshopper*

I stretch my ears.

Perk up, listen hard to make sure.

There it is. Nothing. No-sound. (I can relax.)

Release with the thud of it.

## "Two gray hairs appear in the lit mirror"

The wind howls and becomes old wind, the wind of
    another city.

Yester-wind that once I faced, knees to forehead, in my
    tattered chair.

That was a dark time. I felt close to the snow, its
    unprovocable stillness.

With snow, even in a flurry, there was me, consoled,
    unbending.


## Is it midnight yet?

Quiet deepens. I walk in the moon.

Hushed rays sadden. Their soft half-circle light.

The thought of you emerges. Your woolen scarf. Your
    slender hands.

A northerly wind swirls from the winter wood.

### "Stones are lean, mahogany and NANMU trees are strong"

Bashō, as he lay dying, took his poems for worthless.

This was not just posturing. Words, he felt, who cares?

Yet each day I sweep my room, arrange my pencils
carefully.

Seeing them all lined up so simply . . .


### Dead birch tree, your fungus shelves the snow

My mind grows freer with the passing years.

No patience for the Three Obediences.[1]

But like a giant floating-heart, adrift between empty
banks,

a bowl of wild plants eaten, discarded . . .

---

1. A Confucian dictum has it: "While not married yet a woman must obey
her father; once married she must obey her husband; and, after her
husband dies, she must obey her son."

## "Knowing that friends are coming, I use my foot to clean around the wicker gate"

Why complain of loneliness and seclusion when a hermit's
life is what you seek?

Sparrows frolic, roosters crow, so what?

To be one of a tribe of mountain birds floating by a cliff,

you needn't be a mountain bird.

## Pien Luan's sparrows

O my son. Do you really care about the wind of which you
write with such passion?

The river gulls, the south pond lotus, the north hill that
sends up purple shoots?

Why should I doubt you? (That would be your answer, of
course.)

I, who managed to lose the river's poem.

## *"Icy-skin-stony-bone"* [2]

O Saikō, no one could think that your senses have turned
    to ash.

Your *hakubyō*[3] bamboo take away my breath.

A tree's white ghost with its ostrich plumes.

"We all regret that spring is not longer."

## *Woolly blue, undulant, stark*

Our bitter fight over, I go to my room.

My philodendron, my lacquered chest – what was I
    thinking?

How can I pretend to have my bearings?

The pretty hill, with oncoming night, more and more
    blurry.

---

2. Another name for the plum tree as well as a metaphor for a beautiful
woman.

3. A painting technique Saikō occasionally used to paint bamboo.

*Please don't sweep the autumn leaves that linger
around the well*

"Wedgewood." Yes! Finally, after hours of struggle.

Deeper, deeper, excavating associations, yet the word itself
escapes.

Growing old, I marvel at the irrelevancies that flood my
mind.

Su, I am charmed. Your "three delights"[4] move me to tears.

*A long and firm sweet flag comes from yesterday's
festivites*

Snow hisses down. My fire sputters.

"Jonathan died last May. He was twenty-four," you say.

A shower of sleet bashes against the glass. A green moon
slowly rises.

Caw caw caw. One black crow dominates the northern
river.

---

4. Morning hair-combing, afternoon window-dozing and bedtime feet-
soaking.

from
*RAGA*


Punjabi bells.

Awakening to alms handed through the trees.

She was twelve.

Sparrows of Lot. Bull-red and singing matter.



Pluck. Pluck. Pluck.

Fretless neck. Wooden knobs thud.

Trajectory of me (the king, the sage's student).

His chasuble from shell.

The bowl of my sarod.

A hollow vessel. Gushing dizzily of infinity.

What's me, I say. I stay steady. Or tabloid of Him
(its shaft of hen sound).

Sing a hymn of glory, fox.


Prince throat.

Young hair parted in the center.

Father please (before the striped-cotton curtain).

I want to dawdle amongst the piebald man.

Cousin. Do not smirk.

The beauty of laughter quietly through the flowers.

*Abba Abba* comfort me. Let me rest by your feet.

Cirrus minion (noxious hands) pulling truffles of gas


Peacocks cry my daily *riyaz.*

Bangles and silk jubilant by the fairy books.

A gabled roof, a pane of sole, truce of my ear's solace.

Alone, terrified, aching for the bird.

My little gourd plays *da*.

Raising my chin from the rattan carpet.

Them gigs of reprieve. (A public avowal.)

Sons in triage . . . *shishya*.


Disparate.

Nib of intelligence scour the pier.

I am fed. I grow. I dilate pretty.

But the Ferris-wheel was getting to be uncomfortable.

Banyan of sorrow. Will she cry?

She went to the river (singing bad lands of youth).

Autumn luv. We've had our words.

*Mandir* of hearts. (Votive. Celestial.)


O *Ram.* I (the Talmud).

Maladies of children yarmulke or no.

(Sari-clad) festooned with swags, hollering beneath the
coverlets.

"*Panchamrita,*" cried the deity, mahogany voice cascading
from the poster.

Allure. Her gentle huskiness.

She'd moved, studied, wandered in the night.

This *gharana* (*dosha* of the beaten man).

Troubadour. Wild wind. Shivered the wireless (*gherao*).


*Facing silk flowers.*

Tides and multi-waters digress.

The plait of her forehead, the small of her neck.

I kiss its locks to freshen it.

from
## *DOHĀ*[1]

See the underwater fountain-tree plump with fruit,
    supple and ripe.

Whereby my lama smiles. He planted this ancient seed.

Within each face he recognizes himself.

Swish swish across his *vajra* throne, his immense
    white words spill silence.


Singing, yes. A hundred-thousand verses.

They curl like jewels (amulets of thorn).

Sifting through clouds, clear-mind of enlightened
    existence.

The *Aum* of creation (through which we continually
    regenerate) arises from his astonishing way of
    knowing.

---

[1] *Dohā* (Tibetan): devotional song of experience and realization from the
Vajrayana Buddhist tradition of Tibet. *Dohās are* meant to "reveal the
inner nature of the singer and express her insights and devotion in an
uninhibited and unique fashion."

Shivering reeds. You have been my mothers,
    exceedingly kind, protective of me always.

Glistening flower, butterfly, bee, waxy petals that fall.

A bushy-tailed squirrel surpasses thousands of *yojanas*.

I look out on the bluff. It is brown and quiet. *Lama, hear
    me. Kind root lama.*



To excoriate the stars, I scream.

To placate clouds, I wail.

Clearing my throat, I chant a hundred thousand mantras.

In this way my craving dissolves.

I reach into my mind.

My room of wood is lush and dark.

(My home faces south on an embankment that
    slopes steeply.)

From time to time mists wreath its imposing neck
    like a silver scarf.


Today as I was chanting, rosary beads clicking,

my voice became a bell from whose echo a strong
    remembrance arose.

I am in a hall with monks and horns high in smoky
    mountainous air.

Daffodils cover the ground.

Thus I age and die and see the luminous white field.

"Send me to Sukavati, please." (I pray hard as the
    wise ones suggest.)

A cycle of teachings is repeated by heart.

I hold to my heart.

The pulse of the hum. The tilt of the sky.

Fragile fingers yawn, paper thin and shiny.

Shavings from my gouge trail to the ground.
    Curlicues pile up.

In thinness, absorbed in my ablutions.

For it is written. (Our time will come.)

Fire and flood will ease all.

The gutted slope displays its roots, throbbing,
    twisting, dangling in air.

I know that I am a mountain (that I will continue
    to be a mountain) for three incalculable eons.


I'm beginning my evening prayers.

The nectar of peace seeps into my thigh.

I dissolve into my song. The cry of a bird, my
    primordial voice.

It feels like a cave. A place of no flowers

The sun, with a smell of coolness, sinks.

A slow drizzle falls.

A man dies. But it is not a breach (really).

Jasmine and rose follow him everywhere.

THE WISDOM MIND COLLECTION 2008-2013

## Introduction

Between 2008 and 2013 I wrote a series of eight books, beginning with *The Tethering of Mind to Its Five Permanent Qualities*, and culminating in *The Twelve Nidānas* and *Mingling the Threefold Sky* that are rooted in Tibetan Buddhist philosophy and dedicated to "stretching" English in order to create gaps so that Wisdom Mind might flow through to the reader. The idea in these poems is to not-quite-make-sense. The beauty (hopefully) of the surface language plus the strategy of "approaching narrative" first intrigues, then holds a reader, allowing, in stillness, the dawning of a new kind of intelligence. As a poet, I feel that this body of work is my most important.

The complete text of all eight books in the Wisdom Mind series follows. For more on the linguistic strategies which "baffle the mind in order to release the brilliance of the mind," see "The *Way* of the Poem."

# The Tethering of Mind
# to Its Five Permanent Qualities

CONTENTS

## NEW YEAR'S DAY SWIMMERS

*i*

In fir trees in sky, bathers on grass in no particular order. Towels strewn in no particular order.

Swimmers mostly standing in water, in sunny pool though light is muted.

Muted sounds from low benches at certain distances (air the color of crisp blue).

Clouds, sky, day, in perfect symmetry of day.

Image of boy now fading under water in shadow of darker blue water.

Pale day occurring above cold pools. Day is there next to white water and waders' bird heads.

Is white completely calm (sober) water.

As token of figure bathing and what she *feels* about bathing without reference to motion and breath.

Without reference, motion and breath *are* the composition.

A photographer sees breath as blue shadows on the bottom of a pool. The pool has no sides, no bottom, so it spills over.

Motion is outside breath in language bonded by the requisite of death in the picture.

Swimmers tread water waiting in waveless drift, as if volition (or feeling) is the karma of water.

Death is blue waterless waves in moments of preparing the picture (loose clear bodies of boys in cold swim water; bland postures of bodies wading at water's edge).

Bodies wade *inside* the water without reference to themselves in the water. Only the language of themselves wading.

In time *before* as if wading in advance. Years pass in the person wading before the water.

Proportions occur in composition of boys, water, red-and-white ball and the pool's various surfaces.

An image breaks in the internal place between two bodies.

To place herself beneath the weighty water, being water and the brain of water, is being *back* 'in' water, as in 'mother water.'

Being queer is not being the thought of oneself as that.

Being queer is the same as if one is occurring.

A field of sealed bodies limps mentally toward water.

Is repeated but is thin (what occurs lapses).

*If* she occurs is separate.

The sealed bodies of waders drift off-shore submerged.

Which is not that occurring either as it exists, ceasing and occurring. A length of sea, *down* in her.

Immersed in water—*being* time—suited or in the cold flesh of water. As if time around the water, which when occurring, is being ceasing there.

An Oranda's bulging eye perceives the pale flow of water as *fingers* of water, time around its head.

*Mere* voice spins on its tail toward familiar sense of twisted water, eons of them *wearing* water.

A syllable in the foreground is a serendipitous presence. (Others watching others in water somewhere else.)

One's hands shed sound (the intelligence of sound).

Two swans in the twist of their necks. One's hearing is the silent swans under them in the lake.

One's hearing is adjacent to the sound of them (now lit in slinky under-lake, honks simmering in little shore peep-hole).

*ii*

A year ends below water. Several bodies appear surrounded by gray light.

In portentful time of being *in* the time of that which is as yet unmanifested.

The time of a wave, say, in the advent of sound before it is heard by those with hands in parkas.

Gray dawn as sound is placed on faces treading near-motionless water and expressionless bodies standing in boots at the sea's edge.

Also the experience of facing water is her facing water whether herself inside incipient sense of water.

Hearing is passed through the heads of those staring. Is an expression of sea—hearing form (entropy).

Others say nothing but in their minds is the hearing of those watching.

Which is indistinguishable from sea. And from time.

Water hearing water in the windless waiting of cold day. Its internal sound is an object of water's mind.

The heads of those immersed in water is also sound. One's hearing is also below water.

One is *being* hearing and at the same instant hearing.

One's interior sea is an object and at the same instant the mind that apprehends an object.

There is no silence in one.

Sea and words are sea hearing hearing. One imagines oneself facing hearing as aspect of hearing's sound.

On a plain there is water. Somewhere far off I hear wind or sea shattering.

A person sees direction and space without the intelligence of space (so that she is its mute face).

Faces stare at water being primitive and without location vis-à-vis water's actual boundary.

Water is there, not *for* but *being* repeating. Staring repeats the aegis of a view inclusive of itself.

A body hangs from the topmost place of water.

Inside a wave fades, e.g., there is no interior to the wave.

Yet she resides in 'no interior.'

Seeing *inside* the water's legs which is hanging.

Headless legs stand in seafoam. Others look out being on legs though the dripping in between is dry.

New Year's air is dry and solemn today bent near legs. A sheer leg.

*iii*

Looking through grass toward young sea water. A structure holds sea in and out of green sea-water.

Long slab of gray cold water, bodies lashed to themselves. Nothing occurs simultaneous to itself, in deep awareness of precious-moment's disappearance.

In the barren waste of vast, thin water, a falcon wears sea wild at its edge.

In slab of sea that is Dead Sea, kiosks are seen by one looking at the water.

Seen-through water, a shelf of water. The sense of sea pulled back.

Mind is green, then alone. A girl's mild body holds up like a slip.

A man is thin where he grows without hearing. Thin bird, moving against falling.

Like craziness repeating, a mind realizing hearing (the *stakes* of hearing) in the context of women asleep.

She glances at the sea, though *she* is its body. *I move but day too moves along with its falling.*

The long day slides below low clouds. White lines cut the hill horizontally.

Falling below falling, the falling of day clings, but it moves down the hill like a second pair of shoes.

A slow dog moves slowly with the blossoms' light, falling with day down to the cold sea.

A dog trots through sky, albino skin a beautiful borne white.

It shimmers in a line though it is alone. Other dogs are its borders.

As if she were day, a blind dog stops. At first it is sight, then low sight, then *she* is the sight.

Islands of rock stand in dark blue water made to appear as distant person in yellow vest.

*Do you reside? Do you not reside?* Energy, like the water, is low, seemingly bland, unruffled.

Bather's flesh is real. Mermaid's flesh glows in creamy ground of water, frosty-blue tail, sharp flapper, pointy.

Shadows on walls, like flesh, in passing moments, *is* each moment.

A full moon hangs but it is separate from night and does not spread its light anywhere.

BARN YARD

A woman sees cows from behind slated blinds. (One slow green-lit cow.)

Luminous tiny birds in dark green columns are still-small, low-flying across the meadow.

The sound of a bird is the girl's *feeling*, not the empty bird.

One's hearing is in a mass of birds struggling (invisible scurrying touchable-but-outside the occurrence of their bodies).

Nothing moves (being destitute of hill in 'flat' hill at the ravine's bottom).

Nothing moves. Cuds move in undercurrent of dark motionless stream.

A photographer sees sky/hay/hill as composition of linear fields, muted colors divided by thin bars of black.

A tree's interior edge holds sky.

A rooster crows in thick gray air that rises then falls away rhythmically.

If I can replace myself then, taking back something from before I appear ordinary.

The shame of the familiar, like an ordinary barn.
A slum in light has perfection of the afternoon.

There are lines, she is told, of carefully wrapped people.

People are dead in different colored shirts.

In the sky's translucent provenance, an elder piece of her, crooked in its arms like a waltz.

*ii*

Trees are black in aslant nature of coming together as trees. (Dog in sweet complexion of light.)

A woman eats cheese and says her bread, which is wood, wafts from the mouth of a young girl.

Seeing imbues the loaf with food.

A girl in birds, in black sea light, rides along a canal of light.

I am their teacher so I am hurrying to get there. I begin to run.

A woman eats holding her mouth above her.

Figures emerge in rock moving normally in awareness of shorn fields.

Blackbirds rest on someone's hands in cessation of being in a particular field of sight. (Is endurance of hands or the property of folding one's fingers to make a perch for the bird's claws.)

A photograph of birds are the same birds omitted from their form so that the print is not *of* them but cut out from them and from the cessation of them.

Form without the appendages of form is an image of pure sight (omitting that action).

A red one, say, in skin narrower than herself.

If she's confined letting the skin loose. A girl is a chair sometimes in expanded position of slingback. If she's washed herself.

Where she would be fully sleeping next to it. Feeling its walls.

An empty mouth like sun comes where she does it, though its layers and layers smell like the inside of her body.

His pee in the gush of some riverless doorway there.

A 'we' suspends out, being outside water peeing or inside to feel the warm drift of legs.

*iii*

Mute in sun. Of bare air in day. Dog in sand spreading time through tall blue summer.

A man sees time from before or during himself, days of himself in continuous parallel lines.

A road veers off to unseeable distant landscape known by him once.

Waiting is touching. Still-summer air inside seated person in blank moment of dog.

A woman faces dog, though light becomes something modular.

Emptiness and light compose the luminosity of her voice beyond the composition of any structure.

Emptiness and light compose the luminosity of *his* face. He looks at the grass and this knowledge makes the grass warm.

Trees listen like grass, the *other* of myself, interior line of time endowing hearing with time.

Trees soak through time.

So she's dead. *There,* in morning light. The *other* of time spanned over light.

Not as in death but simply ceasing, though she continues to be alive.

Day falls and if she thinks it is her mother, a bell rings in her skin.

Light falls like a mask while she eats her bread. *I am dizzy with bread,* she acknowledges.

What is the connection between resting as a *place* where light is a place and the immanence of the place like a dark (dissociative) fugue?

What is the connection between her face in the sky and the never-never land of her being my mother?

The immanence of her face, flat as water, though I have never known her at all?

Slowly she becomes my mother. Night falls on black branches of something generous.

HALLOWEEN

A child reads. Winter sun pours through the salon windows.

> *Is that a skull? I mean on your big toe. Can I see your toe?*
> *Would you show my daughter your toe?* she repeats to the girl
> applying peachy-orange polish on her child's.
>
> *That is <u>cool</u>! O my god. That is <u>so</u> <u>cool</u>.*
>
> *Would you like one? You can have one. I mean I'm just saying*
> *you can if you want. It's up to you.*

Oneself as a child with those who frequent the salon being absorbed.
Sun drains from the sky into the salon's flattening skylight.

People are not visible, barricaded off, so that she can be arriving
there, slowly behind her mother.

Her agency cut off. Her mother's agency also cut off.

A man alone gazes at sky. He is writing. Light pours through the window.

Before dawn a man stands at his stove silently filling a thermos. Watching sky someone thinks of him writing. So that the day is expunged with the exception of his writing.

A man writes looking at sky. The day is cold in mind of person imagining him writing.

The gray lug of sky only appears interiorly.

Things ahead of one occurring.

A dog seen from its side is not the dog's profile but 'as if' cut out from its side. The dog is itself, not overlaid on its side.

Seeing the dream's sound, being boisterous automaton of dog overlaid on its side.

Hearing-behind-hearing is simultaneous occurrence of before and after hearing *how* hearing exists cut out from its own side.

The rose is from a former dream. It could be blue. Many windows open, exposed to the sun's heat.

I dreamed the dream *before* dreaming it, standing in sun imagining the rose alive.

Imagining oneself abandoned in the sense of alone on a street with or without flowers.

Its beauty outside the purview of one.

The wing of her foot in dream of blue-lit space where a peacock squanders herself. A nest of small birds also squander themselves. A child squatting before the nest stirs the nest with a stick.

It comes to one there, the sequence of who she is.

If eating there, being ahead of one's thorough eating, her back to eating as in the dream before the tree.

One's dream is not later, e.g., tall wing of peacock squandering is whole (may not be crushed or heard outside itself later).

One remains behind, which is a direction of force. Staying *in* 'behind' as if one were exterior to oneself, in a 'hole' of oneself.

Being 'there'—in the imprint of seized—the thought seized.

The smell of cold as minutes pass.

To sleep or to sleep back where *is* is *in* sleep or dreaming he is allowed to sleep.

## DEAD

*i*

In morning light reading. A woman sits informally, elbows on chair, in square of light from window to her left.

Porosity of light holds resting in silent form.

Day too is quiet like a river drifts, arcs over her hearing.

A woman holds the color of herself, height of room and quiet, as if time and mind exist because their origins are fallow.

A woman in light merges with light which is postureless.

She is young inside her sitting spread in morning light.

A woman in chair is necessarily alone. Shadows bend wood against its destination.

Matter dissolves in undercurrent of herself drifting away from her harmless body.

Is it flowers or my mind emptying of them, though they remain in sight?

She may also be old. Her neck is old bent over a book. (Bathing cap and girl with octopus staring at sand, not moving.)

So dying arises. A viewpoint uninscribed.

A place utterly familiar dissolves inside you. Time dissolves, carved out of snow.

Yellow is how, in the fury of night, while daylight on land is, like a woman in the morning.

*ii*

In darkness behind something, can of something.

A building glows as if it were teeth.

Naming the mother out. Naming her outside beauty.

Like the stillness of a flavor, finding it in an old can.

I wind myself around the can's sweet edge.

The synapse between light and light's real life.

*I am real,* she thinks. Like a gash in sky, a dune is not washed of lit dune night.

From beyond light, the deep act of *being in light.*

It rocks in a tree she fears may be stolen.

So it's *singular light,* its own knothole of light that slips through the flower's markings.

A color is heard. (Net of warmth, through the grass to the tree's edge.)

Wilderness accrues in great spots of white.

The dog is my mother rotating on earth white-skinned.

O she is dirty. Like the end of memory, some form on her body beyond her own grasp.

A tourist at death impersonates someone trying to be her again and again.

Another person keeps her. In latent light the rescinding memory of that boundary.

Another person is a memory of sound retaining the physical latency of having once heard sound.

*iii*

A woman is bare in bare bowl of wind.

Lips green, pain the shape of day. She divides pain into sections.

A man waits for death watching birds' concoctions from their throat.

Fresh wind blows waking birds in net of family bowls.

I draw wind in my mind. Your beard creates little steps for it to rest.

Stepping over stones where rocking animals sleep. (She'd thought the leaf had them also.)

A buzzard begins, swings its heavy, lazy body. *It's the leaf's death. Inside rocking's skeleton.*

It is young-dead, waiting in the coverlet for birth to happen.

A big bowl opens. A vulture easily in distant sky fills around my being.

The placelessness of birth dawns in her mind. *May you belong here. May you swing over from death's outer edges.*

Crickets hearing death grow still. (And underneath, as if the chirps were water.)

Like a fledgling's open throat. A fledgling seeing a flower knows her throat after that day.

*iv*

A word touches you after me and before me.

Something appears blue, scrapes the backbones of this color,
wishing that I am a blue person in the supreme daylight of blue.

The shadow of your word falls against my home. Who you are in the
dream of my mother whose tongue has touched a lighted field.

Rushing sky she will touch other animals who face downward.

So I begin in words. Sitting down and emptying her, like a tourist latent in a guesthouse window.

*Will I recognize her face? (Because my mind preempts her face.)*

Once I forget. I race down the entire dream, imbricated, scales loosely dangling, like the mother-tongue of a stranger.

Hearing forms a line (a column in the mountain whose groin is the mountain).

My hearing is a sea of birds pressed inside their voices.

My hearing is a world shed as a locale once qualified to constellate mind.

Like a paper doll I lay flat.

Her eyes follow my voice, seeing my hearing back to its loosened page.

Who are you mother? Where, among myself, can you plan who I am?

You are born inside my body, lusting after my thigh.

A body parts from where it's left off. An ace or queen, a paradigm which can be touchless.

If you fake me, who will I be ?

*v*

If you appear my image of you shifts. (Not having readiness for a person shifts the mind in which the potential person exists.)

Which shifts the language creating that person. I translate you to being *in* and *out* of your presence and the translation is like your presence within the boundary of a word.

The thought of clean air is a foray toward a word, as if a word were a place for her to store herself. Inside the word's claw.

A woman shaves words picking up one at a time from a little bowl.

The word's 'other side' exists prior to the word.

There is no hearing outside *being* hearing, thinking one's sound is that.

A word's sound is separate from its wordness. The 'action' (karma) of a word's sound being also separate.

Reading sound, recognizing a notation as conveying one's interior sound simultaneous to hearing in one where 'one' is the same.

Outside one is also the same.

There is no same outside time. A sound repeats but it is not the same (though its label is the same). Time doesn't repeat.

A person doesn't repeat.

A crow caws, which may be interior at the same time as hearing in one.

Jays caw. Jays won't eat plums though there are millions of fallow plums.

A line spreads to the indefinite distance altering with every shift of light the millions of redwings on phone wires.

Already her skin occurring in the phone wires, dark in dark night.

The *result*? Sound hearing itself as sound or hearing itself as hearing with or without sound.

A cello at dusk makes the blue sound of a river.

A crow's caw is itself throbbing.

A woman bird struts across the green.

A woman's wooden bird is violet-colored (loud) in the smooth cream of a dream.

Her craw is full (empty of sound) carried in her violet dress.

She groks some sound strutting through leaves near the riverbed.

In the pearls of her feathers is a head being her enjoyment.

The young throb of her body is pure mahogany throb of young bird then (as if birds were, already occurring, in moment before now).

Snow birds in exotic black flap then.

*Telling who telling who in mirrorlike* shaft of moon.

*vi*

One fox in late light empties like sun. (White head in snow spilling herself into us.)

Suddenly swirling so that snow scrapes snow, continuously, like a tuba.

Fingering these years of snow, fragments of snow, suddenly (where I am).

I wash myself in thin night land, like night on a pony, skin scratched of light.

A glint of fog makes them be together in a pile.

A pile of horses neighs, stops in weatherless hill, eye-whites in mud.

Stepping backwards into water, nostrils bleached in odd pattern of children.

One horse empties into red Mongolian arrows.

Washing herself like a black bead.

Washing themselves into white sand.

A meadow is where their thin black shawls dissolve into water. Wild birds dissolve into scaffolding of water.

Water glows flat. A brown girl enters a river in late light.

Among her is a swamp. Now present in a dance as if she is waking (first) between herself.

A girl enters her body first.

Sisters occur. (I am borrowed together with my mother.) As if hearing the cry of her own future child imprinted in her femur.

A fetus moves, birds, trees, former pets.

Wool is made from parallel sheep in arbitrary cubicles in sky.

He sings to them such that his voice is like a large mother's palm.

Here is a lamb from where it was once. (Because she saw him once. Sky on clean line of ceiling, rafters holding up ceiling.)

Though her condition arises from touching, she cannot imagine herself as an object.

He lays the bird aside so that his children may see it but not know it.

*vii*

A proprietor is thin. Her arms are shaped like paper. Which she folds like a doll's paper.

Drawers full of paper are of different weights and textures like a man she knows that reminds her of a city.

He plays horn. The gold in her cloak becomes the color of his skin waiting.

The time of his voice seems separate from the steady *sotto* voice that could be a doll's voice.

She takes place in his legs like the legs of her husband. (Legs fold in manner of his countrymen.)

She thinks, *Good. Now I can be like a line moving forward outside present time.*

The edge of her in her clothes is so thin it might break in her clothes.

Not a fetish but still knowing that the fetus is buried.

A child breaks up. Is intensity not-yet-worked. (Repeatedly becoming an object of *formed or shaped intensity.*)

A brass's ethos retains. It places anywhere in a formerly-worked object.

Hearing the stark name of a previous person. One may write the person.

Entering memory (an object in her mouth), ladling it up, placing it slowly where it belongs.

Your willowness enters song. You delicately twist your hair to a feeling that's like a country.

The pain of sight together, now in a specific setting, where a person's capacity for song (metonymy) fits tight.

A dog gobbles flowers. Space retains his passing.

A child waits, like weeds wait for flowers, retaining the passing of former names.

## THE PALLIATIVE OF MIND

*i*

A rock drinks an animal's life, easing it into the mountain. If a sentence goes on, it's her mind stringing pieces of her eyes.

Seeing the movement *before* the animal and hunt and hunt, as if its skin were alive.

*Before the air, that was the air of the people, lilies were private flowers,* she was thinking. (A flower's skin may be public skin yet lay beneath private air.)

An eagle turns, *repairing* air, like a squirrel turns to face a flower, as if some band affixed him to the flower and he is sure it is *that* flower.

The gallop of a squirrel is mixed with air, *carved air,* yellow like cowslips.

Throwing itself after air (but the cool flank of air). *I know air already,* you murmur.

The way light hits a flower or stone at dawn. Night *behind* night, blood in sunlight rising.

An animal, young in sky, washes back from sky. So I memorize sky, at the same time *think* of sky.

Wind becomes sky, light through distant tree trunks if sky were there, or, light with trees with no sky allowed.

A bird hops on grass, *weathering* the grass, leaving little igloos of white.

Lines of a bird grow down the bird. *Will grass survive its wing's blue tip?*

An old jay caws but its caw lacks the shrill, coarse modulations of a jay's caw.

A bird in flight brushes a flower's head.

Waiting rests as day passes in the flower's knowledge.

How the day as it rests admits further day. Like a flower is alive and its secondary life, encapsulated off, will not be allowed to overflow into it.

When the day ceases to be day because, you say, *it's fixed,* I know this.

A quip of birds from the far river rise. A hill slides into the valley's dark night while someone reads pressing himself open.

*ii*

A gull circles a wedge of water, marking the water with her eye. The memory of her skin is limitless, like the memory of her cry, before a kill or later for the sake of others.

Wind, too, gains qualities by its forcefulness with things, its *hand,* say (a piece of sun cut off).

A crack in light, like a painting of light.

*The palette of wind is gold,* she mutters, *the boundary of a man playing chess in light being the dead person.*

A flower emits voices behind falling sun.

A flower is soft and the pain of soft reminds her of a sea of heads.

As if her life dreams its own violence. If a bird disappears, she may have asked for this to happen.

She begins to think that mountains wash out mountains. That the sea of heads form a land on which to walk, which she calls the *isthmus of larks.*

So a bird flies flat and what is it about its sleek blue mind.

*Is a bird a bird or quality of place <u>dawned</u> by the bird?* you mutter.

You look at a chirp, though it could be surreal. A tree *comes* just at the point of sky.

Phenomenology of the tree rides not so much on the stature of the tree but like the tap of a cane, where it goes after it is hidden.

A sycamore branch in late light sheds, as if sun splashes scattered shards of larks through needles of light-fall.

Time is little drops like from a spout drip-dropping the bough.

*Its stem is underground,* someone says, and I have a memory of a double stream flowing deep beneath the earth.

You tap on the stream to *awaken the stream* so that the leaves stop shaking their light out of it.

*though actually it is the same earth*

*Rat Dream*

An old woman is born. Her hair dries and her
mother thinks, *I have been her mother again.*

Might the woman's nature leave? Rats scurry from
baskets, which are old baskets, hexagonal fields.

A night bird sleeps. Its dreams are down to its feet.
Which you say is the bird's body before the skill
of the bird's body.

Its wings lay flat in the smell of new grass.

*Commentary*

A quality of him, *home words* say, is the same as the
man speaking.

*I already have that person,* I think because his blood is
smooth also. My blood is smooth also.

A person moves, effortfully or effortlessly, and she
thinks, *Is this a waste or not?*

She thinks it is bliss but *thinks* it is *her* feeling bliss.

Is *filigree* air, like in the rats' playpen? What can hold
  between a feeling and a queer girl child whose boots
  tips curl in shame?

I am really talking about rifts, what holds between her
  fear and the rats' miserable-life fragility.

There would be an object connected to my playing, like
  *saying* playing, as though words are desire.

The likelihood of death browsing itself into *my* death
  could occur and I think, *O yes. It <u>is</u> death!*

Each word has a flower. The times of the flowers
   converge so that she conflates words and flowers,
   *speaking* flowers.

Pansies in sun beneath the red breast of a robin, here
   and there, merge with the robin's legs.

A duck in scattered ripples darkens. snow falls, resting
   in a petal's shell.

An infant puts a flower in its mouth. The muscles of its
   mouth move by the flower's warmth.

Rats kneel to her and in her mind become true rats.

*The weight of the snow is heavier than words, heavier
than stone,* she marvels.

*Is the Christ child born of air, through holes in the air?* For
the blood on snow is real transferred blood, alive in
the mind of the boy.

The beauty of a rat *depends* from its limbs. Snow folds
and the boy becomes its eyes.

*Cow Dream*

A double flower begins in the folds of an infant's hands.

If you see its face, which is the fruition of your
    knowing, it may be a small, infinitesimal aspect of
    knowing.

*The fetus is standing,* someone says. She imagines her
    hands under its armpits. She spreads it on leaves,
    which look like artist's hands.

Wrapping purple leafy fingers around its bits of unborn
    life, she climbs a person inside the lark's mouth.

The fetus shines and she takes it to school. *The forest is ill,* she says. *Anything tall makes my blood quiet.*

A series of events moves in one direction only, like trees taller than sky.

A woman sees a bird and thinks something about its eyes. A clean, fresh feeling becomes that feeling regardless of her initial sense of affection for the bird.

Roots are veins ripening in her body though still hot as coal. This is why a bird's cool blood is the most delightful fowl quality.

*Commentary*

In the ether of white my baby fumigates.

The flavor of her skin holding a flower to her nose. each
    particle is a bud and inside the bud's head.

Flower and water are protectors, with the net feeling of
    white, as if a lotus absolves its entire color into her.

*I made my baby backwards,* I say. I am trying to
    remember if the long lowered arm vibrates.

Trying to recall time, my baby, offing of morning fields.

Young rocks sit like cows in sovereign pasture squares.

Or you may instantly be the baby's wisdom mother, the
   stronghold of you and your baby going somewhere
   pretty.

A spider's thin web zigzags into sky, whereupon the sky's
   dimensions shift.

If you appear, my image of you shifts. Not having
   readiness for a person shifts the mind in which the
   potential person exists.

Which shifts the language creating that person. I
   translate you to being *in* and *out* of your presence
   and the translation is like your presence *within* the
   boundary of a word.

When you appear, the interior land shifts making sounds
   like stones.

A spider's thin web zigzags into sky, whereupon the sky's
   dimensions shift.

Later you say, *a spider drowned*, juxtaposing your seeing
    with what you recall.

But one imagines tall black trees or a cow that hangs in
    privy to the cow.

*If I see the cow with you, but if I see the cow alone, we*
    *have to know where it exists.*

If a cow eats air, the air still exists.

Each and every cow jumps over the moon properly.

Meaning is the experience of one cow, before dawn,
    slowly traversing the earth.

A falling star holds up the whole earth, so that its drop
    is a pin-prick against water or color.

*It is my mother born from my body,* I'm thinking, while at
    the same time seeing faces of other relatives.

*Tiger Dream*

Sun from behind the mountain falling on the threshers
and reflecting from the lake gains depth from the
sound of falling.

The sound of water over stones at the lake's edge is like a
darting bird.

If she wakes, she couldn't say the bird disappears, but its
breath dissolves, like an undertow at sea.

*How igneous (fiery) and lucid are the bodies of tigers,* she
muses.

*Commentary*

Each day the sun slips over the crest of the hill and
   lights the yellow grass.

A cat climbs the hill as though dawn were in its head,
   entwining pieces (petals in branches).

A day-moon slides below low tide. Fall-out from one's
   skin protects it from further harm.

Tide emits tide as she wanders down the coast, empty as
   a battered jug.

A woman carries a jug dexterously embroidered on silk.
   The woman's skin shines like the interior pink of a
   river.

The dimensions of the jug's magenta is implicit yet
   exacting.

*Out* is not a direction but an aspect of conference
   around the jug's battered aggregates.

Bringing yellow *out,* where *out* is a structure of color
   *and* light, intensifies *out,* as if its DNA changes.

There is an hour in which her memory will be there,
  where light falls in rain on a tiger's flickering head.

A stone woman prays, hearing sun in sun. (She dreams
  its *precise* nest.)

A magenta flower glows so that I feel free at last. A
  magenta flower glows, disappearing in its skin.

Light jumps back as if she has that person again.

Death is color-added-to-color.

Color *learns* color by touch, like the *feel* of rain from
   one's bed.

What if the occurrence of harm refers to the difficulties
   of *offering* the harm? In the broad space of an
   animal, a wound in a woman's thumb feels like
   embroidery of jasmine and honeysuckle.

The necessity of something and its form *is* the tiger
   sleeping, tail to tail, in tandem with something.

*Hare Dream*

An angel glides silently through air to where the child
    Christ sleeps. He sees her as a crow, wings folded,
    watching.

A blue flower in the wing of a bird hovering near the
    birth, is not *in* the bird, since it fluctuates in light,
    while the bird remains unchanged.

In my mind there is a bed where I drop off.

Christ and hare both slip through my mind and
    land where a hare might or where someone needs
    something.

*Commentary*

The bird whose markings fluctuate remains unchanged
   independent of its visibility.

Yet her girlishness has continuity. *Limbs jumbled in the
   corner are still free limbs,* I'm thinking.

All the animals are resting. I know them from the inside
   as if they have *said,* and their word is a death-rattle.

A golden crow or laughter is said to be a paradigm of
   activity then.

So there are words, then under-words.

Black words like a river so that her thoughts,
  pummeled, are the hard thoughts of stone people.

They burn a branch of all their people, then turn to ash.

*Am I the person? I am the person.* I decide I *must* be the
  person.

While a glistening star holds night within its skin, a
    twinkling star has no interior where night can sit.

So she lays with the animals whose foreheads quiver.

So many ducks and goats being *causes,* songs where
    voices are *tongues.*

Sweet air sweeps the ragged flowers. sweet air sweeps
    her hair. (Winnowing its hair is also an object.)

The beauty of the straw in the wake of a bird flown
away. As if the whole world encased in shadow-
brought-to-bear-upon-a-field *stops* the straw in
time.

I'm thinking time occurs separate from the straw, *beside*
the straw, and in its looseness is neither created nor
destroyed.

Seeing something *against* time, as if time were *old-
fashioned*. A shoe, for example, is eligible to loss.

To be dead again, in the simplicity of its skin. I hear a
leaf and think it is in the well, so we are together.

*Dragon Dream*

*It is just beyond her body to sleep with him.*

*It is just beyond her body not to sleep with him.*

This is the moral of a little play. There is a lodge.
A young girl is invited into the main room. She
is black with very bushy hair, dressed in a silver princess
costume, carrying a wand. She comes in and behaves very
sweetly to a guest but her parents think she is faking her
sweetness and really being sassy so they ask her to leave
and come in again, this time being genuinely sweet. So
she comes in again behaving slightly differently. Each of
the two times signifies a different moral.

Commentary

A doll talks and if she's a tall doll, *in dependence on a listener,* her presence will not disperse far.

Her body covers her life as if it were a cast.

Mop-like braids fall to her waist. *If I were a Cyclops forging thunderbolts, I too would be being born* she posits.

A man binds his mind so that it doesn't scatter.He tucks it between his breasts. *How have you left your mind before?* someone asks, speaking politely.

After long rain a man leans on a gate. Hair-thin legs
    race along the rim.

A disappearing chirp *has* appearance, like its body is
    young yet forever carried in its old mother's womb.

For her presence *gives* also. Her feet and ears also.

She grabs her limb dangling in the breeze like a cocoon.

Cobwebs in sun are strings of pure time dangling in a
breeze.

Cobwebs in shade land, decrepit before time, cave into
time.

Part goes up. so that time feels like war.

Another portion rolls into air—holding air, lighting day
back.

A whoosh of wings feels like an effigy, some sort of
    charcoal beast fluffing its feathers, eating sky with
    upturned beak.

If what is visible close by is remote, vast visibility, I
    inhabit my thoughts more fully.

Inside is a stage whereas outside is somatic. A great
    slaughter of beings is contained within their death.

As if a holocaust is *found,* as if future beings *trip.* Sky
    washes sky as I watch a dragon fade, wings rubbed
    by sky's shadows.

Snake Dream

A woman seeing an animal sees it belly-to-earth *raised
    above the earth so that it floats on a small peninsula.*

A python, like a bladder, coagulates the sludge, eating so
    much sludge.

Light from its eyes shoot out little tails of fire and she
    wonders why its death seems so friendly.

*It dies on the highway 'cause it's slow,* someone says,
    thinking of sand. It vanishes in squares, *as if
    striations of sunlight are old.*

*Commentary*

My mother is dead. *How could she have forgotten her*
　　*shoe?* (A hazy memory of a dream where I'm a
　　colorful bird's tail.)

She sees the bird hop and its hop disappears into the tail
　　of the bird, into the tails of her children.

*Here is a whole bird,* she thinks, *its tail discrete like a*
　　*discrete word.*

If one dies, among birds, a red-winged bird is heavier in
　　its body then.

Caught in her own heirloom of light, a woman sleeps in
  distension of moments that appear to be there.

Old birds swarm. Quadrilles of people (fitting the crate
  around the edges of her body).

Immersing herself in a log. Some say she *is* that thing,
  as if she hops inside it.

*Mother, I am blind,* I say. *Your pink toes reveal nothing*
  *any more.*

A yellow fowl touches logs contingent with animals
who knew the logs as sky.

Of previous people drawn on the backs of stooped
women. She felt she was that woman. That her
yellow earth bloomed in the night oil.

Afterwards there are leap years then. Like fields of
potatoes.

A child hops, square to square, with her own
convergent yellowness.

The emotion of yellow, say in meat or chirps. The same
level of color in the blank place of sky is like borders
in sky mirroring the bottom of her eyes.

*Is it painted?* a child asks. Her sewn face has alterity and
depth.

Pink is here and you are *sure* of the color. Before being
born, grass is this color.

To bring back sky, it *pulls* the sky so that sky folds
comfortably over everybody.

*Horse Dream*

*Where is day?* someone asks, and I see the twin
     nature of black, oil of black, mountains stark and
     wet.

Pearls seem brown like the bottom of the sea.

I whisper something and the animal's ear flicks. So she
     lets her leg give this impression, a pearl in the dark,
     in the blue of its stomach's shell.

The mare's perch is illuminated because blood and
     ecstasy are to birth like an underlying river.

Air rushes in, steadying my mind. *Your words are my mother,* I'm thinking.

Long legs curl around a shriveled coil of knees.

An insect wanders off. It's a baby I see and my heart breaks for its infinite slow old non-knowing of direction.

*Just get through the line. Get to the yellow snow. To the bridge where you can puke. There. To cut yourself out.*

*Commentary*

The sky frames your face and all the different skies.

You're the crow against the sky or quadrants of an
    insect's shell from the perspective of sky.

The *place* of you is like the essence of your eyes.

So you're blind, sort of, and another person sees the
    tension of that space, the *acoustic* opacity in that
    space.

She may know a sound but if she turns, it becomes a
measure of far and near distance.

*I wear sound,* someone says. (The slimy pearls are the
physical sensation of womb.)

The woman's space, lighted by sagebrush, transcends the
confines of a life, though it can pull life
toward it without abrading its transcendence.

She wants it to be white, like space in a word's world.

Pearls are steam. The lug of its knee or inside the beast's
thigh.

She may see blossoms, a sprig, or she may see pearls as
old mothers marching.

The blue horseman is blue light, though we're, through
it, seeing death.

On a bodice is a pony, which drips into me, until things
become small, but they still die.

Watching-minds twist to a cumulative suicide. A
   windhorse flies but it is *still* still, asking me.

*My daughter is young.* I see her climb inside the
   windhorse, her long fore-fingernail painted with
   geese.

I determine to seek them, over the hedge, inside the
   parts where it hurts the most.

*They only read lips in the blinding darkness,* cries a priest
   from behind a screen.

*Sheep Dream*

I have a memory of green, in a hole, in a moon's crater
    called *the bottom of the pitcher.*

A woman fills the hole with crenellated wings. I admire
    the wings so she cuts off a piece and hands it to me.

A man's voice held anterior to its space makes his
    presence real. *I'm not cold,* someone says.

*Is cold an image like young sea blossoms, purple flowers*
    *just above eye level?*

*Commentary*

I recall seeing myself in a dream with the sensation of
something touching my toe-bottoms.

The dream includes a variety of skin sizes. Certain
shapes whose edges contain sky, I clearly remember
in my hand.

The skin of a lamb is irreducible, like the skin of day
bound by fleshy rock and sand.

A day may not be prior to itself, happening alongside
each and every event of breath.

Shells on the cowboy's coral hat are new surprising
    shells, shiny, polished, with no sea showing.

I forget the boundary of possible seashells while
    holding the thought of their appearing in my spine.

An appearance occurs against an old barn door. All
    stags as they are burnished beat their heads dry
    against some tree or other.

The parity of their body is the parity of voicelessness.

Flinging off his gossamer, hanging it up to dry, dancing
about the pan, *drinking* the pan.

The memory of the color green is tinged with repeated
time like little beats with a glove.

So I *learn* green. Whose solemnity is sky (*view* as, say,
sky).

I look at green and become an old woman.

I *chew* green and the rich saliva gifted by him.

Is a *tenet* of color, a *primer* once left off.

As if the person were a taste congealing inside her very
    own wisdom.

I drift within its skin, an opaque membrane of light,
    allowing pale color to metastasize.

*Monkey Dream*

A flesh-colored pear is with the heaviness of birth.
  I look into its head wanting an immaculate black
  stick.

The pear tree has birds arranged in its branches
  artistically.

Here are flowering birds, whose trees spin into air, her
  feeling for the blossoms, sharp as thaw.

Monkeys race, seemingly, though it could be bones
  rolling and disappearing.

*Commentary*

How the weight of a bird hopping along a fence, a tiny
    bird new to appearing, not yet carrying the birdness
    of its mother.

*The more anchored the mind, the more an appearance*
    *weighs nothing.*

Light is bone. think recumbent, dead-seeming, like an
    animal playing but really guarding beings.

Fossilized wings show the giant wingspan of an early
    species.

If a bird eats a worm or if it turns its head, an animal
    sniffs age, sees age in the pattern of its feathers'
    colors.

Cells of color leak, wandering over the wing's rough
    neck.

The flesh of the bird appears in its hop, its last place of
    hop, what's possible before lifting off.

An animal gauges the belly of the hop trying to
    determine the feasibility of killing its hop's dark
    past.

A young bird stares and something birdlike travels
    upwards.

A mud-colored bird blurs into mud throbbing there in
    her mind asleep.

You could say she wears feathers and the feathers
    unfold like a resplendent bird catching its reflection
    in sky.

You could say there are rivers, battalions of orange light.
    A child spears light, ravishing light laid out as in
    death.

Seeing the feather of the bird through a branch in noon
   sun, one remains in the bird and is swung, like
   through an opening in sky.

So that there is both the bird, belly like an urn, and the
   bird so saturated with birdness that it is unseen
   against its own background.

A group of feathers on the same bird, for example, are
   separate and distinct yet we think of them as the
   bird's feathers.

The arm of the bird is crooked. In skinniness in sky.
   Distance is its face in the resting sky.

*Bird Dream*

Three birds move in air as blue as water in a dream.

Three branch-colored birds land on a branch in the
   borderland of the bird's robe.

Behind the songs of birds he fingers a chip. *Is it thin?*
   *Without the chip's color?*

Seeing its form as a bird, first eagerly then angrily, the
   way beauty through a gap in sky breaks into two
   whole containers of sky.

*Commentary* I

An ebony feather shines, its blackness steely, like the
   hard black knuckle of a bird.

A discarded feather, arched like a fish, rests on the
   earth, its magnificent bow gleaming.

Sun-black birds hover over sea, so that black is both
   inside *and* the holder of itself.

Or like sea repairs to sea, *wraps* bird and sea into
   something apocryphal.

The time of the bird is *ideal,* you say, by which you
   mean *supremely excellent time* and I think, *Are
   time's qualities measurable?*

If it were touchable, the parts of a person might
   organize around it, like one's senses congeal around
   a smell.

Bird clouds drift. Sky too seems to be drifting but it is
   still, I assure myself.

I am comforted thinking the sky is still.

Time enters the wing of a bird where the colors break
    between blue and very dark blue.

An animal waits allowing time to sway between its belly
    and inhabited spot on earth.

*It limps,* she thinks, though it is a genuine limp, with
    each and every particle of limp belonging to *it*
    specifically.

In a certain angle of sun she is able to see the limp
    passing to a future animal at a similar spot on the hill.

*Are the birds girls?* The impact of sound makes slowness
   material while its *direction* is immaterial.

Saying it is less like looking than a cloven foot with
   little clea's or talons.

And maybe she is that or maybe her body is simply the
   thought of a bird-filled body.

Later I dream the three birds are crying. *Fingers of hair
   blow with the wind,* my mind observes, referring of
   course to the talons.

*Commentary* II

Three bird's bodies whose bones are like a forest. you
   know its color from the pure knowledge of color,
   without seeing its precise color.

Lines of light catch the bird. The motility of light
   critiques the contours of the bird's beak.

Part of the air surrounds a branch where three birds
   rest. Rays of light touch your back, which, if I touch
   you then, evaporate.

As if the boundary of your back were hidden by your
   back, but nonetheless yellow, like light in a dream
   person.

The profile of a bird, in a gold ball rising, *shapes* a
   mountain called *bird mountain.*

A crow erupts, turning gold turning curves. I cannot
   tell a crow from the image of gold feathers
   somersaulting.

The bird's dream arises from the ground of its own
   birdness. First moonlight on rushing water, then
   pink stars like angels, then tree tips in a treacle bar
   of sky, threading itself through the birds' raised
   mouths, beaks pressed apart like lips.

A thin sun crawls to earth and is maintained by strong
   earth, though actually it is the same earth.

How a beaver floats under *sky-words*. He *hears* the birds
as if gathered together verbally.

An end-bird leaves its formation over water. Its blue
bowl leaves, rising in sky.

Which somehow was known, the way a line is known
as beginning *here,* though, as you say, *lines are
concepts.*

How many meanings flow from the bowl into heads
that look away?

*The robin's breast is red,* you think, yet you are
  unsure and think maybe it's a color that *contains*
  red but is not red.

Caring is present though you cannot find it in the bird's
  body.

An insect the bird eats enters the bird's blood. *Is its time*
  *the same? Likely not,* she thinks, since an insect eats
  and the food slips away.

A dragonfly on cloth (conspicuously beautiful)devolves
  into your eyebrows.

*Dog Dream*

I walk into a meadow and all the dogs' mouths open.
  Presences are out who remain unseen and may
  instantly slip inside.

A witch flies out but it is just a stick. *Mommy, it's just a
  stick!* a child cries.

A woman tells about her smelling, it being equal to a
  dog's when she was pregnant.

Crickets chirp in a field of rabid ones. Their intervals
  are pure, like the pure white flaps that poke from a
  new bird's tail.

If a dog is my interior ash force, it romps the hills with
   butterflies sitting there placidly.

If it yawns, behind its tongue are beings sucking
   flowers, looking like black ghosts.

Behind its tongue a world of beings cook. *Its unconscious
   is preserving food,* you say, but I think it's making
   speech, readying itself for a life.

A string of dogs hangs in sky. Daughters of sky gather
   cobs. Hussies also wear cobs.

*Commentary*

A dog in grass hears a young bird chirp and inches
    towards it. Hearing, but not seeing, one bird, then a
    group, early, as if the sky were nothing.

Or as if the sky were intelligence, like a presence that
    the birds knew about, but if you looked there'd be
    nothing.

*Another offers food, but I am offering something more
    gentle,* she says.

The dog's belly is in the grass but its ears are inside the
    hill.

Each day a dog returns to its spot on the hill. Its body
   rests but its eyes are vagrant. (By vagrant I mean
   slim—*the eyes of a crow on a wire in rain staring at
   wet grass.)*

Rain gathers above low hills, like rain in a painting
   stays mixed here.

Like the footprint of the doll, once left in a storm, has
   neither situation nor destination.

Five children laughing pull grass to the river. The air
   around it blurs, emerging from weather.

A bird and dog move, appropriate to pleatless rivers of
    air.

A bird and dog sit, appropriate to the posture of all
    birds and dogs, *which is genuinely sweet,* she guesses.

The time of the bird is not the dog's minute-to- minute
    watching, though the bird hunts from the sides of its
    eyes.

A dog has parts, which each have times, so that a *melody*
    of time pervades its movements *and* posture.

Posture, too, is a way the idea of an act is projected.

If it is blue there is a door so you *enter* the posture,
    though the light *in* blue might leave you suddenly.

The dimensions of a star are not of a star's body but are
    fixed in her, displaced by her movements.

She moves and the star achieves its posture.

*Pig Dream*

A longshoreman sees night. He looks at his hand. As if
  night or water or distance were simply depths for
  the color blue.

As if night were still night only very far away.
  The appearance of the color and its instant of
  apprehension is nothing more than an action.

Before the action the color doesn't exist.

*Where does aqua go?* she wonders hearing flowers
  falling, falling where they adhere, into a world
  of tea.

*Commentary*

I am today again. I fall within time, tall time in a frame of
   tall pieces of color.

A bird's red wing releases the inside of its color. I
   look inside. *If blue were there, its wing wouldn't*
   *exist.*

A teapot's rhythms are cascades of water falling and
   I imagine that I too am falling, in strands, like a geisha's
   hair.

*Is it the lines or the openings where things recede, emptying*
   *themselves out?*

Being moved she falls and I'm thinking it's a young,
   fluid sort of fall.

*But air is internal,* she thinks.

*O mother of sky lugging me forward. You break off but
   I catch you.*

A voice through fog portends the precise ominous
   chartreuse where your eyes look out.

When you see blossoms causing a two or three
     dimensional image to form in space, your eye opens to
     that space.

Space, she thinks, exists, crosses back from where the person
     was alive.

A bloody bird from the beak of a hawk clicks the
     nature of night. Its cry is her face clothed as a human
     bird.

*The blue of a cross pinned to the mountain.*

Thoughts divide into lineages of translucency,
    sun-dazzling corruscancy.

I define *grow* passively. I point to a flower and say,
    *That is a growing flower, unlike its shadow*
    *spidering sideways.*

Now she belongs to an infantry of animals. Packs of
    pigs form cover near the kraals.

For example, a girl *thinks* the hog, but tells her mother
    to draw the hog.

# Mother's Warm Breath

## CONTENTS

# BOOK I

*Birds*

**Once I saw a bird**
still and pink
standing in a grove of trees.

At twilight, on one leg,
growing thin
like a very young girl.

*Might it catch a bird, swallowing its bones?*
Its vessel holds sky
carrying sky to a different place
where it is fresh.

When the birds blew further away,
she felt the sky with her hand.
The gray corolla of old ones,
on a washed-out hill,
colors broken off.

*How old is she?* I ask, but they are sobbing.
A woman watches,
remembering herself through the bird.

*Rare beauty is begun,* he thinks,
seeing into the hill the limitation of my seeing
where the dead person lingers.

*It is myself,* looking at the grass,
seeing its kindness suddenly.

Food is offered,
though a throat could disappear.

*Every given moment that you perceive is the same thing,*
you say and I'm thinking, *It's the bardo.*
*It just arises and you see.*

You throw a piece of cloth on the hill.
*To see if the hill has green in it.*
Then you rub the cloth,
gently touching your fingers.

Sometimes the cloth is wrapped in sky
and when you touch it to your face,
it moves jerkily.

The hill is seen from the belfry,
its transparency of light
merging with the green motion of air.
Light crosses light
on the edge of their fur.

The latitude of fur
as a place for light to rest,
each hair being a *support*.

Husky wings in low night.
In low fur.

*Blue is blue,* I'm thinking,
*separate from mirroring,*
*blue or a mountain*
*or a person's face.*

This face is my own face.
The slight sound of a bird
fluttering in a bush
could be bells
or roots like cascades of long fragrant hair.

A vulture scatters flowers
and I saw that she saw
that the wings of birds
are light-fields.

**And now it is night.**
Seabirds play in frothy chips of glitter
coiling like an aroma
that is not one aroma
because fading light gathers
*packs,* fish, flies.

Bone-buttons in a bowl,
like lotuses in lakes,
drift behind her mind.

A rabble of dogs snarl.
Whose limbs are dogs
stiffened in their tracks
or crooked trees
dwarfed like a witch.

There is fear
and the notion of drifting across,
as if a button is a raft
pulled by sky,
little awakenings by little awakenings.

And the fire-pink, its ontogeny,
how it came to be, as you say,
*erupted.*

*An Avalokitesvara appeared on the bone of my foot*
*when I took birth as a dog,* a monk says.
The time of his bones
or sweet hair falling
on the muscles of his shirt collar.

You wander around
from dream system to dream system,
listening for yourself
being handed to you by someone.

Is like air being handed to me
by someone.

The time of sky has no direction,
no containment,
is and is not a vast field.

She looks at the hill but sees
the logic of the grass,
a memory of death in a bird's harsh call.

What is *behind* the grass
*erupts* from the grass.
*Is* in her, as *is* in flesh.

A bird purrs and its heart drips
as the color of night thaws.

The flesh of the bird was broken that day.

Which wouldn't hold its feathers,
as the flesh was *keen*.
(Old ones said *provoked*.)

I see you on the edge,
a fissure or cleft where a breach has been made
and I think, *Am I the breach?*

The gestation of wrongness is not carried by wings
nor the deep drop of cliff
overhanging the swollen stream.

**Being in the dark with so many mountains,**
so many startled animals.

*Please don't try to tell me*
*there are animals in the sky,*
someone says as she dozes.

To affix a buzzard's beauty.
To stay born and follow the animal's trail.

A huge white edifice
from afar looks like sky.
*Why is the sky white,* she thinks,
not realizing.

An animal rests,
luring her and stroked by her softly.

*Were I white,* she thinks,
recalling the knockered door of a nunnery,
whose square of light
crawls over sand.

In the distance other people are stroking animals,
pouring them in a jar
or vacuuming them up
in a little tube.

I suspect that their voice
*still blends with the night's stream,*
like the trees and
like the real body of the people.

Or like an old nest simply left.
In things said *back*
in the voice of a stranger.

A woodpecker's peck
may be connected or not
depending on her emotional needs.

The boundary of a bowl leaves its edge,
its age in lines
around the bowl's broad hips.

A word in time creeps through its own wet structure,
sentiment (throwback)
or some anachronistic nest
that slips away from its structure.

All this time studying the dunes
that crack around the sea.
An animal is dead
and breathes dead breath.

Is still as a cross
at the edge of a white field.

*I dress and wait for death*
*though I am already _in_ death.*

Through the wall
a delphinium *wears* light,
carrying it to the people.

**An animal eats, rubbing skin against sky,**
so that there is a larger sense of
*being* in sky.

As if it'd been alive
for that moment of passing.
Wind pools hills, luffing,
and at the same moment,
passing.

Sky holds the animal up.
*What holds up the sky?* she thinks,
watching the animal's hands
resting on its stomach.

The animal moves.
Leaves move, and grass, like blowing hair,
settles closer to the earth.

A squirrel flies through air
and the angle of light through its hair
is like the ribs of night.

Dawn in a squirrel
is a raindrop's fresh earthiness.

A squirrel breathes in covenant with something.
A fizzy motion of air
blurs her vision of its claws.

Whether or not it is from
the sweet squirrel's hair,
her trouble of hair,
inside its shell of hair.

His experience of his hair
versus her experience of his hair
in the moment of his jump,
though she is further from his hair.

The non-location of the feeling
later reifies in a dream
of rainbow-feathers on a stick
and a man waves the stick,
touching her forehead.

You almost know who she is,
yet you do not know her.

So you cannot forget her.

Rubbing the bird,
stroking its hair so that it is soothed.
The old ones receive until they realize *I'm dead now.*

*I am half ghost. I eat all of their hair, always.*

*Someone belongs here,* she thinks,
having the memory of her mother's hands.
A bouquet of birds
contains her mother's feeling for color.

The hair on a fly, motionless,
contains the memory's breath
clinging to the hair
before it disappears.

The hair is not an image of sky
though it has sky qualities
and has come from the sky.

A gallery of eyes has the willowy look
of lost people.

A shadow from the sky
holds the hills apart,
like a tuft of hair
emptied of sea.

The beauty of a fox,
its pink quick speed.
Wisps of hair, air-brushed.

**Each night the sun slides out**
below the clouds,
behind the *sun leaning.*

One color leans and the other leans,
so that there is a clean surface
for the air to move.

The rim of her body moves
like the rim of an animal
twitching in sleep.

Now I regret my voice
in the trees of them.

A woman lives in her neck,
settles in her neck.
A cloud on its side
is a vague motion in her heart.

Night lashed on its braid
folds around her back
like a shell.

A bird's neck is infused with life,
but later, after its song,
she does not see the neck
and thinks it is inside the bird.

Geese prefer milk
in this extreme world.

*Ah, geranio!* someone exclaims at an osmanthus.
It is November. The rareness of sky, wind, birds,
in the month, in the sorrel
and clay rocks of the past.

Two doves nest high in an oak.
One sits on a branch.
Engorged with sun
the horns of its center relax.

I see death spread sun around your arm.
Empty snow-light
like a glassy puddle of melt.

The nipple of the bird,
its sound in the dark
and thud of its fall through the cliffs.

A butterfly lands
so that her face pauses.

Hearing the bird
she follows her mind
into the tail of the bird,
into the tail of its children.

Hearing the bird
the occasion of its air
and complete *symphony* of
chromatic features.

The delicacy of its wings
as the deity pours flowers.

**Awakening in snow you hear birds.**
Their call is deep,
rising from the riverbed.

I *hear* your face in the
echoing of trees.

Bare branches on bare ground
like quills in cold night.

Each emitted word
in the compost of earth fluctuates.

Seeing the stark barren word
flicker like grass
covering the bird or
place in the meadow where the bird grew.

Your words are mixed with flowers.
Mermaid words,
half letter, half calyx,
drawls the mind down.

Like a word may be breached,
or *defoliated,* she says.
Its skin waxes blue
across the chain-fenced field.

Sometimes it slips from under itself
so that virtuous, non-virtuous, neutral
maintain in the word
*after* it is broken also.

Then her words are the only true words.
(My own experience
were also her words.)

Awareness deepens to a pool.
If I feel each letter,
the heart of the word will be calmed.

The impasto of color,
of her face and of stone.
The course of her face being
*before* the face,
so that someone else,
seeing the light,
could arrive at her face.

Her approaching her,
*before* her,
its existence as an ache
rising over the top of the hill.

Ultimately birdness is a very primary,
bottom-line, open-ended
sense of awareness.

Experience is what arises in awareness,
the way light, say, accretes
across a frozen pond at dawn.

Through the wires it is done
as when a thing has progressed
beyond being erased,
beyond a point where
it can be forgotten.

You are *marked*
and for how long in this sky,
reposing on a col on the summit-line.

**A hummingbird in air,**
whose qualities, imbued with dahlia,
*sits* in air
independent of the dahlia's redness.

Simply seeing the flower's shape,
discovering its motility, *qi,* or,
as if wandering about,
its intrinsic comfortableness.

*I'm lucky,* you say.
*The brand of the child is mine to keep.*
(You can see the furry flower
hugging its own passionate surface.)

An insect's leg outside the flower's horn
dissolves in cold winter fire.

*We are one sky in ourselves and in sky,* she thinks.
*Sky is air changing into shapes of sleep,*
*but it dies into sky,*
*gentling itself out.*

Air is thin then,
feeling through it to her breath.

*Is there a place, like sky*
*or inside a flower's head?*

She knows the town of sky,
*slow ice of all sky.*
A parallel sky, like a mountain park.

Your face holds sky and when I look
I see a particular old sky.

Gestures are like sleep.
The pathos of trees stroking the lake
with their leaves.

A woman wears red
in the tall lean elegance of a bottle,
as if her shape were identical with the bottle
and also an old bottle.

A drowsy man walks, carrying logs,
so that in sleep
the sound of their falling enters.

Red leaves cover death,
the substratum of death,
the materiality of blood thought of as *her* blood
or *her* past.

You are started.
You begin in my mind
before you are you.

Sometimes rabbits and prairie-dogs
scamper among the grasses,
but hers, now dead, would be found
among the leaves.

An image—*a chameleon's green in earth*—
comes before or after the image,
as if you could peer through leaves
to the war in the leaves.

**Being thin, I see mountains.**

Shade within shade is where a horse sits,
but internally, like shade
crosses a person's eyes.

I live you in my body.
Is not ahead of her body,
as a woman lags in her body.

Wandering around ahead of her large body,
a woman reads and the words
take place in her ribs.

Teepees line the land
where she sets up her drums,
in eggshell light,
thin with beautiful pale colors.

A jeweled pheasant drags the wind
and fog is smeared through the pebbles.

Her crimson wing *(still in the limb)*
lays on wind,
relaxing the wind.

Sun floods a leaf
battered by weight.
Swirls slowly down.

Sun mows *down* into a bone of air.
A person notices and moves
with a slight 'reflect' motion.

That circumstances repel.
That there's resilience in a
'reflect repelling instant,'
the gambol of repelling
now in a cloud
on the clearing's north ridge.

Each time you climb a piece of sky,
you are imagining it is sky.
Vespers are said in a chapel on a lane
and the words reach the road
but do not stay in its memory.

A body lingers on the road,
then seeps through the road
draining through the aquifers.

A child climbs a pole,
beside a string of birds,
beside the waves hanging there.
His ladder to the sky
has no reference point.

*Come sky* he writes but spells it *cum*.
The cum of sky,
the sound of birds scuffling song
through evening weeds.

Rainbows, sometimes regarded as dragons,
appear together as double rainbows.
They soar into the sky,
*mani jewels* threading from a string.

Cold lake, for thousands of yards,
soaks up the sky color.

**Once there were birds**
damaged in the flowers.

If you look at the horizon after the bird,
the memory of the bird
or red, where the river flowers leaf out.

A bird sings strong
and her *will to sing* is strong,
though it frightens her.

Her will to sing becomes a branch where she sits.
Thus singing loses singing.
Subsiding.

How dusk fills the tree
is how the child's weight is borne in her.

Its feelings are a bowl
whose qualities come from the base of itself
and is how it truly feels about itself.

A bird sings and as I look beyond you to the bird,
my mind follows my eyes.

But if I gaze and my mind wanders somewhere else,
something shifts in the figure of a pigeon
I remember touching.

As if a pigeon were a natural replica of itself
so that seeing it
is seeing dark.

Holding the bird,
sheltering it in my pocket,
its warm life drains into the fabric of my sleeve.

Seeing the flower in a mirror
and the emotion that caused her to see it that way,
a little death.

Whose attribution is not an appearance,
is not opaque,
but fluid like a wall or statue made of butter
in the still mind of a soldier.

Flower is flower *and* time in her mind
out of darkness.

*The end of sight is clear dogwood,* he says,
where *clear* means empty
and *dogwood* the clear light of space.

A lama moves and I see his quiet ribs.
*My grave is made from logs*
*so that night will be left there,* he says.

When the dogwood becomes earth
we say the flower dies,
but a child leaves a meadow
not its life in the meadow.

# BOOK II

*Sky*

A woman rests. She is lying on a bed back-to-back with a seated man. Touching is there but its *time* is not there.

A woman rests *between* time. Like time in special settings and she is the setting whereby time vanishes.

So he *paints* her body, being invisible and also seated on the bed juxtaposed and contiguous with the other person. He paints space though it looks like figures on a bed.

The woman's experience stretches toward the man but is unknowing of the man.

I see light in the interstices of her body contracted around
their crash in her body.

As if shadows cover the hide of sky's body, the concept
of sky's body being a short cut in time back to the experience,
*opposing* the experience.

How sun against the grass continues to the sky, the
enclosure of sky, like seeing encloses sky,
*sky-before-sky,* and the hour of sky's *midst.*

A sapling touches sky or exact moment of sky as philosophy
of *this* sky, beholden to no other sky.

So there's sky and my experience of *being* sky, opening my hand, letting time be one of sky's animals.

A woman at dusk is green because the animals in sky are the color of the trees.

As if there were sun in young green sky so that green may grow wild.

A pool of birds on the bayside rill, the knowledge of which, the absolute utter familiarity, not of birds but of birdness drifting south along her orchid's lips.

A feeling begins. She might have been asked to teach this feeling, as if birds learn feelings once they wander from home.

Like the sleeve of feeling relating to the sleeve of skin. If she notices, if she sees the bird seeing the feeling arising in her, transparency for transparency.

The relation of a sentence to a bird or words to *things* (a word exposed in the skin of a woman cooking, knowing something not depositable in the room).

A bird is light, being light-in-light, or air, in light, in water or air-in-air, like a line around air.

Shape slips to shape. *Slips is for life.*

Sun rests along with the woman and her chair, the fluidity of time crawling over wood.

How light against wood *pulls* the woman, *wing of chair* affected by the pitch of the wood's fire.

As if war were there crossing a line of hunger.

A bird begins, *darkly flying out.* Someone sees the bird and thinks of Icarus falling as if falling is time and a boy falling is a measure of falling's resonance in the person.

A woman *hears* the self of herself falling, from the *inside* of falling, outside any limits of time.

Passing it off as the *performance* of her falling, her experience of falling outside her experience of *feeling* falling.

Angling its falling and the scattered tits of its breath's loose scabs.

A boy falls in neutrality. Between the *feeling* of death and death.

I *have* the person, I say, instead of when he was the person, as if the person were its birth, and also, the experience of its birth.

Being *hey* in the spread of a corpse's tail.

We strain events through time as if age is a place jilting her to there.

A cricket squeaks, objectifying air, seemingly.

The mystery of its disappearance in the dominance of a breeze, as if breeze intrinsically *contains* squeaking.

Yet an eminence rubs off. Light alternately occluded and revealed.

A cricket faces east though it is unseen and comes into east slowly.

Even my mother disappears in the red carriage. She waits at the side of a snowfield in her hat, which is an elegant hat, beyond her capacity for a hat.

A hawk skirts sky along the places where sky stops.

As if place were not the hawk but all things touched by the hawk.

A caw is like space, gluing space where caws are space.

My mother is a cloud like day across a hill. *Hill* is an agreement.

A being's short life, without the *affection* of life stirs a memory of experience exterior to what is beheld.

Like an offering thrown *opposite* the sign where a negative force originates.

The lines of my hands sink with the sun. *Who may you be crawling where I am, dangling from the riverbed?*

Sometimes I think that my spirit sleeps in water flowers. *I sink into the land spreading like a shadow.*

Violence exudes from the flower's previous color as in her mind she cannot find the color.

Something sad, say, may look to you like a color, like fate is a color.

Seeing is *conveyed* like a boat conveys seeing, seeing death and then its color. Seeing's inside *is* color.

A woman begins, though her face is absorbed, dark in a
dark room.

As if dressless, a woman reclines at the bottom of a space, perfectly
alone.

So a body grows down into itself, which is how a painter can paint
himself and not *be* himself.

Seeing the inside of time, the *constraint* of time, like a flower in a
cornfield blossoms into a puzzle.

The beauty of air, moist, and her experience of moist as she breathes night, in and out heavily.

As if a shell forms inside both of us. The shells of her are lines turning light into a quality of time.

Density holds time like water in a lily congeals (sets) so that a cause happens and the result looks like a lily.

The pinkness of time whose insides are flowers *is* in things, shells smelling this way.

A bird begins slowly, is *risen* slowly.

A vague line of mind annuls the feeling in a word which is replaced with lines of time tracing the word's beauty.

Time appears but it is color not time. A bird's loveliness is time.

Slow is the horizon itself.

# BOOK III

*Mother's Warm Breath*

DOG

My old mother barks. I hear her over death.

*Wake up,* someone says. A letter dissolves into the being's feathers.

All the little animals *timed* to her, playing we, playing the arms and legs, so that there isn't anything left.

The portrait of a dog, its perpetual yank of teeth is a portrait of *dissolve,* where *dissolve* too is liberated from what's false.

The brain of the sound loosens into color.

*I, a dog, claw myself out of solidity.*

Her toenails are claws and she gets to choose which kind of dog.

As the brain descends, darkness descends, in the *no-house* where the dead assemble.

Is the claw a bone? It seems to weigh more than the bone.

Like the weight of a bone being suddenly too heavy, as if her body were the wrong body though the bone is okay.

I'm trying to remember. Wings are divvied up. The track of one hovered in a spoon.

I dedicate something, which sounds like a word but I am dead.

Fades in a distant dog. There is a waterfall. Dogs fall into her body.

Fades to sea (kerfluffle of brook) the mountains and rivers of that tidepool.

The wingspan of a dog has white speckled markings and there are *heavenly dogs* which she painted.

The jiffy of her dog, *o my god,* in its quick march toward its drumbeat.

Someone whispers black, which is enclosed in black like in a wedding of black and me.

Since its aggregates are black, I call myself *black* and sit in it like a dish.

The sound of day stops. The wooden dog stops.

My hand is me now. So you can't tell. No one can tell.

HAIR

Her mind is hair, white, earthy, cropped, like *total hair.*

*Give me your hair,* someone says, which I think is my mother asking for my hair.

Offering hair on a platter, the sound of a plum sits in its color, as if the stomach had her name etched on its flesh.

Ripe and dark, like the rind of her being scraped and
tossed away.

It is the bed inside her mother.

*Mommy!* But the bed is a plum in which the mother insists
she sleep.

A thin bed, fragrant from practice. As if her skin were too shallow.

Which could be food from the settlement of her father.

A hair is fed. An offering of hair yielded to the mountain.

A youngster bird grey in the mountain. In its plum,
spooned up and *being*.

The bird of hair speaks and it is a warm bird, as if air could
be a bird, the *wait* of their tongues having never before
been brothered.

My voice and your hair thrive on a metronome of waltz time.

One fixed to hair. For example nuns, in the white folds of wandering hair.

Which the nun hides in a shell, so it is there, with her as she washes, and she knows her hair thoroughly.

I, the voyeur, do not perceive her *hidden* hair. I *may* not and *do* not grasp this internal shield.

I, the voyeur, am outside the circle that her yellow hair makes there.

I *intend* hair, I say, and begin to practice those qualities that support it.

I mean from its depths, like the nondiscursive mystique in the drape of a nun's habit.

You are allowed to be hair, bottomless hair, through drapes whose folds hold the depths of hair's feeling.

I lay upon a rock, ministering to them, to the empty linearity of her mind exposed on a hot day.

SKY

I make a connection between my mother's *towel* as an object and *towel* as the nature of my old mother in morning sun.

She grooms light in the endless cleaning of herself.

She bends over sky. I *draw* sky like a lesson of myself.

From outside through a window, an image of her in split-second segments.

*What a filthy piece of sky,* I say, brushing the air with a spoon.

You feed sky to the person. A leaf through her skull
blows down the valley.

She recalls something, the dead child's face, or more liminally, think
of a still-born's face.

So sky is subjective, like a private game of cards, shuffling, dealing,
from the bell of each card.

Sky is an *ability.*

As if there were a zoo of sky, a rib of sky inside the bird.

*At large in death* inside her own emaciated wingspan.

I *hug* sky, the *limbs* of sky, mimicking fruition as in starships.

Being an angel then, in my own hole of sky. Now I am gone but we still talk, don't we?

Now I am not. The bone-cake of me gone.

*My old mother's bones are quarter-moon bones.* (Whose butter bones suspends from the sharp essence of her breast.)

Sky stops for a moment. Or tree of sky which I experience as a cuff of sky.

Eagles rest on it. Are forms projected outside, as if they exist very private and wrapped up.

To ascertain the rhythms of sky your fingers tap to that.

As if the mind of one were a baby. On the shore of herself, as though time itself, as though time were *there* running alongside time.

Time is color then. A capability from the old river.

## PIGEON

A girl steps out of her tall black dolly. The mother of one, like a doll plopped in the corner.

Where is her prettiness? A certain prettiness that you know, that you can even touch.

Soft breath from her eyes, but the eyes themselves are rocks.

A songbird peers, caws. A fish caws to the harmony as if it knows who it really is.

You are the person that you have forgotten. As if the real you fades into air, indistinct from the particles drifting across your face.

Where waking sees ground and you are the ground, not dead wood.

Being privy to ground (king of ground). A young bald bird sits parallel to the window.

The hill inside the bird. (Knowing the hill from seeing the bird's shadow.)

A bird bell tolls by the river of her father.

Wrapped in a dress she tucks her wings. So she is just a dress. If you look you see a dress plunked on a step, asleep.

Tucked in her dress, tucked like a bird. The spectrum of her inside a chilly bag.

But her feet are young.

The pigeon is immovable. She rests inside me, looking through me to my daughter.

A bracelet at her feet is like a rock carved with her tongue.

So I wrap my tongue in bandages. Is the hawk's wrist in mountainless dead-lands.

In the feet of our voices, the feet of the birds are calm.

Inexorable coo, are you bleeding?

The harp of you, though the monk swore you'd be spared.

Seated in its knowing, its face in shadow is alive.

So I forget who I am. As if the need stopped.

## MOTHER'S WARM BREATH

i

Mother's warm breath, like a *plate* of breath. Yet it is old breath, having eaten many crackers.

*My breath is a wall,* she whispers from *real* breath, instantly present to birds.

The energy of the animal appears to be experienced internally, its breath (a shadow) withheld in its own stem.

What's left of mind as a squirrel leaps out?

If she pulls air out, in a tantrum say, or *superior air,*
parceling it out to descendents.

*I feel the sweet journey of your air,* she muses. Swift and
stark, its transmission in a jar.

A harem of air bustling down the hallway, a *trance* of air
parting through itself.

*I am cleaning my air,* she's saying, as if the air were inside
her stomach.

As if the air were blood and she is poured into a glass. *Air is definitely blood,* someone says.

Warm green blood from the mittens around her legs because there'd be a war of dogs, afterwards, in the bushes.

To accrue war she saves up the *noble green color* because *pure view is always seen through the light of the five colors.*

*My nails are on fire,* she says, seeing her hands in a later version of hands (like being friends with her hands when they are dog's hands).

*How many hands are in the dog's hooves,* she wonders,
because paws are everywhere.

As if all the hands were grabbing her tits greening everywhere.

A birdhouse of tits so that the feeder-birds chew green blood from
the mother.

*I am ordained in blood, the* samaya *"blood" whose liturgy
I've accomplished.*

*ii*

My mother is a *place*. And a being from there having qualities, as if she is also from there.

From the inside of her being her, gradually becoming her in the same taste as russet-pink.

Russet-pink is a field carrying one's pure essence, like a whiff, *oh! that's her!* Maybe some pawmarks.

Totems of her gaining belly from herself.

A place is by chance (like pain is a guess).

Like a lid with its definite jar, she's attached to this, thinking maybe there's no other jar.

The lid has a slogan, which she wears and thinks it's not right if her family does not.

Like a *birth word,* say. *Every person has one word.*

Held adrift by old old hearing.

*Don't touch you!* says her own face. (For she recognizes the previous resentment and its marks on her old face.)

As if spring follows summer and we are already at the beginning.

If my father is murdered, does that mean I am dead or (like *one's face in sound)* about to be dead?

A legacy of light is separate from reflection, like a legacy of dog only sees itself.

So there is mourning but not knowing. She could be a dog thinking she's a dog.

Her formless growl cracks like a flower, like shards of voice but one hears only the thinnest outermost skin.

I harbor myself in the familiarity of something, air, leaves, peacocks running across a field.

People coming in like the last second of her knowing.

As if she'd snapped her teeth. *Stealing* knowing, she becomes simple.

In the interstices of a plan, like knowing skips to what's there anyway.

The value of her in the real actual sitting down, till she rests.

*iii*

It's a disclaimer, the notion of a dog on the outskirts of
her own dog.

*Her groin is young. Her pointy nose brings out the animals.*

Her voice has tongues and the tongues also have some. The muscles
in her tongue carving my name fast.

That's why I die, sipping myself away.

Being old and cold, living in a box. I pull on her tongue so that the air can be colorful.

*Can you fit into a word?* I ask politely. (It is a long thin tongue.)

A droplet of rain ripens. Where is the daughter of this body?

Are *boxes of tongues, postures of tongues,* juxtaposed and contiguous with one's internal experience of tongues?

Her name begins in the back of my throat, bubbles in throats, like a cliff of throats.

In the *fro* of the dream, as if beauty were beyond it.

I look closely at her throat whose little hairs wrinkle. I saw them be calm.

A stream of heads are throatless and I begin to think, *SHE STOLE THE THROATS.*

I, mother of a word, am also mother of its flesh.

I, mother of a throat, cannot know its container.

The ebb of a word still in her mouth. *Whaaat? Whaaat did you say?* she'd say, as if lugging the word up.

Her *whaaat* is space, each letter jettisoned from crayola.

# White Bird

CONTENTS

*First Grandchild*

*1*

The Jambu continent is called the Jambu continent because a fruit of the great Jambupriksha tree fell into a lake, making the sound "*jam.*"

As one thousand buddhas will come and the teachings flourish, this Jambu continent is considered supreme and is called "*The Victorious Southern Jambudvipa.*"

*This continent contains twenty-four great lands, ninety-nine small lands, three hundred and sixty different clans, one hundred and eight remote areas and one thousand and two extremely remote places. The Land of Snows is one of them.*

So hovering in a row, the breath of the row in its high peak of rows.

Squares of light are cool settling night in a row.

The hill air is cool, like a tower of air carrying through to nothing.

Each night the sun yields its bit of darkness to the child. The darkness squats and *plays* dark but the child knows that it *is* dark.

The child counts the *pieces* of dark unsullied by subdued and broken darknesses.

Dark is solid but is also its own lamp. That's why the sun is dark.

Each night the sun gathers its arm. Each night the sun electrifies the sky as if sun is sky's fathomlessness.

*Like being awake in your blood <u>before</u> it is your blood in the subtle state of <u>not</u> being at war with sky,* you mutter.

Clouds of crows carry sky back. Should I, quick, whisper in one's ear?

Each time one dies, one's breath, like the moon, hangs from a *hook of sky*.

Like a leaf crosses a twig and he waves the twig. The twig had already been waved though.

To sleep in oneself, as if one is alive, but not really, only until something happens.

As if the clarity, the full-on *bindu*, amortizes itself, emptying itself, as if the leaf too, wheeling from sky, drops from the *throat* of sky.

*2*

Then her speaking image of a person catches fire. In my dream a man is wearing birds and my speaking image of the birds . . . she clearly sees the long stream of qualities pouring themselves all over his body.

A woman eats holding her mouth above her. *You are tall, and your mouth, too, is a tall, lean mouth.*

She longs to be near what she's sure she remembers knowing, as if an image has an ear and it is *your own* ear so you want to be near it.

Like the sound of her birth in the far-flung distance of birds.

Because the air is there whether you're awake (or you could be awake beforehand).

Whether before, occurring as in the darkness of something. I mean *before* the crows, but the dakinis have already taken them.

If one's mind clearly holds what *is* previously, to recall how in the past such things exist anyway. (Like the woman washes her hair in a lake and the lake nearly dies.)

It knows me in its eye. If I part from me, the rape is left, but the eye stays inside my belly.

So much water making her a person, like a bone in water is the slain inside her.

Instead of her own, she is *their* hair, the skin of her hair being *mother-hair*.

A portrait of hair tucked in one's mother, *as-if* it is *her* hair not having quite left her mother.

A woman locks her hair. It falls inward and she feels the falling inside the hair's cud.

The *her* of her hair is not in my fingertips.

The *her* of her mind lacks the valence of my sorrow.

Lung and tail, I consist. I *am*, I say.

I am in the boat of me.

*3*

*I am her. I am her.* I think it is my mother saying something in a dream.

She sleeps in *her* now, but it is the *memory* of her, not the person *being* her.

Thus people see a form's endless slipping, like a tour of herself drifting along her bloodstream.

At the *foot of air* (like a bloodspot in air) or is it the real air.

*Is that death*, you ask, because the straightest line is death.

So much down deep as a spring morning.

When she wakes it is still down, so close to her face, further and further.

I'm trying to remember that particular mustard-color, like a blood-bath of *down*, stand-in for all *downs*.

Birds grow down. Each harp of down, each plucking twining chord of down's interior pause, so that I *am* (in the pause).

A hummingbird dissolves into its own pure form. One thumb moves as if venturing towards it slowly.

*Oh!* the mother dolly begins, but it is a pretend mother. (However there *was* a possible mother, I mean a mother exists who could be her mother.)

The *real* mother, whom she'd not yet met, would not have said *Oh!*

The beauty of sky relates to birds flying out of sky.

At dusk the hill withdraws into its form. (*Through* birds, quiet has a mode.)

*First grandchild is extreme,* I think, as a mode's emptiness accrues.

*I am that,* I'm thinking. A tree lashes night to quiet, then falls away leaving the quiet naked.

*4*

Being the person dreaming and now, saying hello to the person
who, in the dream thinks, *I am also the dream!*

Dreams implode inward and multiply, like a virus, sort of.

The belly of the dream sits in its plate as if the mind of someone
were growing from the plate. *I am eating for my plate,* the mind
says.

*I am my own faller, being in my mind my own kind of falling. Death
is in the center.*

Being the person dreaming, though dead again. A mind *thinks* but is dead.

A young bird falls as if from the sky but it's from the water where sky was.

You hear the drops of a being, then each piercing droplet of being's time.

I *feel* her sky in the mass of me today. She *smells* the inside of me today.

Empty becomes empty-in-the-mass-of-me-today, like a bone gets loose and falls away in the rain.

A stream of fish crosses her heart. One drinks her milk and is appeased in its fish-ness, like a baby fish would be coming out of its shell.

The baby is frozen. *Not many war people come here*, she's thinking.

Blue is raw, the ocean like teeth. (Inside the teeth are the color of the teeth.)

If a dream implodes and then its bits of dreams (I'm thinking hounds of sky-hawks flaring their wings, *tooting* their wings almost.)

Even without the wings there can be an experience of wings, but she prefers the sound of her mother's skirt is to sun like the breast of the sea buried in it.

Because the things that we are turn about and become who we are.

*I am definitely your mother,* someone whispers softly, but it is just my voice as if far away.

*5*

A bird's song fills the morning. Between song and morning there is space. Like she could draw an ideal of the little bird's voice.

So tenderly green, so *now*-green. A bird doesn't speak but its motion is stored in its body.

*How will I know*, she says, watching the bird see its own face.

Seeing itself there, nipping at air, the traces of itself still in air, like a grike, say, pushing the bird *inside* its air.

Seeing the brain of the face. So much medley tearing up the face. *Each person must unwrap her face, <u>memorize</u> her face,* someone hollers.

*It's like a belfry,* you comment. *A ring of bay and little sips of sky knocking about the water.*

It's hard to say if the air falls away, the lure of *away,* behind the fog (what's actually taking place).

*A bowl of green water may be placid tight water, but it's <u>me</u> being tight, <u>accomplishing</u> green,* you whisper.

Air leaks from her bones. *The last moment of air is the thinnest air,* she's thinking.

*I take my thinness seriously,* he says, placing his mother in a bowl. (As if an animal blows away and is found on its back in a bowl.)

*Air gets tired,* you say, but if you clutch air, mauling a poor, tired section of air.

A dull green bowl holds the water of my air, because the mind of the person is a *trilogy* of air told through mother-air and father-air.

*You* in my air on my birthday cake sighing. (Though I did not. I was only sighing for her.)

*You* in the village of people-less thought searching for that connection.

*The gist of a bird is the animal of its relatives.* (She could see its ochre bill and the young tooth of another new child.)

A symbol of one's animal seems to slip down her fingers, crawling over them also (*and has its own animal also*).

*6*

Each night the trees slip into sky becoming themselves.

*Does the grandmother exist?* She sees the sky weakening back.

Her creamy eyes bulge, slipping back to themselves. She imagines the trees rocking.

Trees light passing tips of sound. You watch them disappear, like a man walks back to nothing.

The lips and teeth of wood hang quietly in grandmother's face. *I am wintering in me,* she says. She doesn't want someone speaking out loud.

Time is exposed. *Grandmother!* I gasp, but it's a heart gasp, like her death.

Within the death are letters. *If you harm the death,* someone begins, because a letter is flesh, beautiful as a peacock.

Her breath too might swallow itself. So many rings lapping waves of sorrow on her broken dress-buttons.

See an eating turkey seeing, the pebbles of its eyes weighing down the sky.

It's because grandmother's skin looks tight. Her eyeballs are too poppy like she sees through time, whereas I don't.

Seeing the ignorance in her skin, its reticulations hanging. The crevice in her mind, its wrinkles hanging.

Seeing her shape press itself there, like the mud of a bed of a river.

Her heart, too, imprints into her skin, pressing its shape into the room.

*I may find sky,* she continues, forgetting. To me her mind feels *brushed.*

*I am fine,* she says, creating a support. *I am fine,* she repeats, her wooden gaze lasted to her. (*Fine* is space so her mind is protected.)

Grandmother's body's *space* seems heavy. Sometimes she leaks out. I say *leak* because, later, if she moves, aspects of her do not move.

*The Elements*

EARTH

*A tulip's knowing is from before knowing,* you say
mildly. I'm thinking, *That's time. Like when Khyungpo
Naljor displayed the five Tantric deities present in
his five chakras saying 'From now on, never see me as
ordinary, not even for a moment.'*

*Time is your own mind,* you repeat, and I have a
memory of myself disappearing, not in death but
somehow being me another way.

Like I'm me without a precedent, as if your body is you
in the name of a foreign person.

A *spring* of dark lingers in time. It was time before
but now the boy draws time. The clear beauty of one
whose color is the *great color.*

To hear the evening sung in night's dim peace. I am
me and then the person who is really me.

The traces of her (or *bowl* of her) like she could be that
and grow into someone saying *hello* to someone.

The collapse of yellow altogether unnerves me. Like
the sheer end of yellow. *Time seems to be more like
that, or the feeling of time sticks on you,* you add.

*It's just whatever you see the world, like a childless
person sees, actually, what is being passed over.*

One imagines time folding back into the cliff. Death,
as a figure, turns into a rock, though its flesh is soft, pinchable like a
human's.

Behavior takes place *after* its occurrence. I move and
am aware that I have already done this.

One imagines time dripping over the hill. She hides
inside, feeling *hill* into its space, so that all her lifetimes
happen together.

Only when you are completely through it can the ink of
"hill," the swift calligraphy in its soft Western
snowfield, become a roaring *geshé-like* blessing.

WATER

A junket of fish is in the crook of a man's mind,
so circular in his mind, as if the world, as if his mind and
the world become the dawn of fishlessness.

Far and near, like the junket is *as-if* versus the smell inside his head.

So many fry wandering around, *as-if* eternity, the
transvestite, is just more precise fish-hood.

*As-if* one transmutes the fish's consciousness to a Pure
Land, which is just an aspect of *my* consciousness
seeming *as-if* far away.

The man bites off its head, mumbles, then throws the
fish toward similar headless fishes.

*As*-if its distance wakes me, like the throes of a cloud
pressing space into its shape.

The memory has shape and the shape time. Distant
and close merge in the fish, which has *duration*.

I mean an imprint of time settles in its skin, *as-if* its skin
*had been* that.

*The fish is ME!* (The afflicted mind is an inward-bearing motion.)

Nevertheless, as the fish recedes, the ilk, all the ilks share the same essence.

My raspy throat converges with the cut throats of that fish pile. *Rakshsas wandering through sky enter into people's throats,* she recalls.

A residue of fish coats the skin of my throat and sometimes I feel I am not my throat.

I am longevity instead. Because someone prayed.
Someone saw the pile of fish's bodies and prayed for
their long lives anyway.

*Mercy lasts*, you say flatly. *The fish enter the divine is
all.*

The man who cut their throats knew the precise
consequences of his action, therefore his assiduous
practice of slicing, tossing, eating, *as-if* his belly were
a globe.

*His belly WAS a globe*, you say.

FIRE

An island backs toward night. Thin slabs of shore and
soft eyes heaving toward these.

Am I dead? (I am nine birds.) A quarry of birds drifts
 in fragile evening sky.

A lion mounts a yak washing back through sky. Sky is
a floor and the two animals are flying but they are
really on the floor.

When lambs are in the sky meowing, each lamb *is,* a
cross passing over the water.

A bird is poised. She rocks her space gently.
She offers her tongue to taste what is held off.

Because she speaks in such pure stream, her *gaze of*
*tongue. Each and every blade of a zinnia is me*, she sighs.

Swarms of arms lay at her side. It could be death. *I*
*am the stomach of my death fallen to the earth.*

Embers of me are held in sky's arm, but *which*, which
arm actually slides over the horizon?

A bird or fish toned by where it flies, slips into its landmark.

A graceful bird, its lip chewed by its mother. She reaches to its lip, chewing passionately.

*I try to chew passionately.* (That is how she instructs her infant birdlings.) *I want to be kind* is said by the mother.

The mother of my lip, I lay awake wondering if she is happy.

# AIR

*The razed town is part of a wall now*, I'm reading,
and I *know* that really the bones and eyes are me only the
book doesn't reveal that.

The skin of the town is injured, which I carry. When
something touches my skin I feel both the present and
the past, the way it *feels*, taken by itself, without
anything added.

Animals are there. They recall their skin. Some
animals scratch, as if they could scratch the knowing
away.

I see a being and know that it's me being that being in
someone's time that's simply slower than knowing.

*I am always dreaming time*, you say, as if tenderly
knowing the color of your grave-clothes.

One forgets that it's knowing. A thought presses
through the ridgelines of one's hand (the silence
inside one's hand).

Like a monk *knows* something, which could be light or
snow or lilies but it doesn't matter because his teacher
sees it also.

When I press on light there is a thought inside, just
beneath the skin, like subcutaneous knowing.

Sometimes I hear a sound closer than my skin (the *distinction* between me and the skin). *I definitely have never heard this sound*, I'm thinking, all the while knowing absolutely that my skin has.

*If you look at a flower then close your eyes, you definitely know the inside of the flower because your* citta *has assumed the flower's pattern.*

*So if you forget the flower you can still have it, like you can crawl inside the flower.*

*If your* citta *is alive, like a rooster in a field. Each dawn the freefall of wings.*

SPACE

Now it is summer and cherries are hard, nubile on-the-tongue.

Now (as in India) I climb a *shed* of sky.

A bird eats a worm near a tree, but it is space, their
host, the nucleus being the passion of one.

Walking westward in sky, where home is a plate of
sky. Howsoever I walk, the stride of space is one.

A woman in my dream walks briskly down a hill and I,
a cornucopia of space, am overflowing with little
horizons of spaciousness.

The space that she wanted was the space inside *her*,
that she would see say in a tree, the way a branch
gives way to sky.

A bed is spread beneath the tree, wider and deeper
into the tree.

Each night she looks out on the hill and if the lines of
sky land quietly on the hill, in integrity with its grass,
she feels she is *dreaming* grass, maybe being *inside*
the grass.

Huckleberry Finn also. Floating down the river he feels *inside* the river and when he is wholly inside, his breath stops.

If you envision light at the point of the *trikuti*, the small light there that enlarges more and more, as long as you visualize that amplified light, the breath stays stopped.

The gross perception of breath leaves me now. Farls of nothing leave me starved.

Death is a *place* and someone *goes to death*, as if going is the non-going of an echo.

*The Fourth Part of Air*

You look at the sky through the tusk of a hill and a cloud disbands of scattered ones. A songbird chirps. The cry of a dog turns to sky.

As if a nerve from sky measures her appearance within a context of light settings.

A leaf unfurls, then fades into sky. Space is not sky, even though she's dead.

A bone of sky (one, two, three line up as skies), a *wheeze* of sky as if gotten out of the desert.

A bird touches sky. It seems so sure. Sure displaces sky just at my ear-tip.

The space of my dead mother is a content of mind, a shock of *rest* fallen from sky.

Birds click sky toward the *perfection* sky. In their space are flowers falling.

And after rain the full bare sky, deep black, like a sea of shells.

I see a woman in a brace and the brace holds her up, but the brace is just breath.

*I am definitely what comes out of a trumpet,* she's saying. Its echo is like her whole mouth. Movement inhabits her whole mouth.

It slowly slips down, though the girl in the death house, she's too thin. Her death is too *there*.

Very tangible air (*cloth air*) arrives in her there, in the fourth part of air, breathing her back to air's non-air.

A woman sits alone. The lines of her life spread. Her body waits for air to tip.

The branching off of age grips a person's face. A certain opaque color inhabits it like a lake.

There is a hat-bearing person. What I hear is the hat swinging from side to side.

The flesh of such greens. Like crushed paper in a branch sweeping ground-cover into green.

My mother is a color (she could *grow* her color), like if a
bird constellates in the blue of its color.

As if her face were on me, a faint breeze or burr in the
side of the dead one.

In other rooms, *under-rooms*, a glimpse of her death in lieu
of *knowing* the deep accord of her own death.

The candles of a shade breathe the word without the
illusion and the breath of us exchanging ourselves.

So I laugh and compliment a person on her color. *What's that shade?* I say and she says *marigold*, which is SO beautiful.

She is wanting to *tell* the color, but is it the *real* color?

*Real* could be a color. A woman sees me, an impression that doesn't erase her image of me.

*Now I am real*, I'm thinking, as if *now* contains the moment that that can occur.

*Am I alive? Maybe I'm just space. I am an interior walking through the door.*

*The time of light may pass,* you say. *Light may fall outside its space.*

A lattice of light, a *pod* of light, gobbling space, or not space, light's *taste.*

You locate the light in the undergrowth of darker ones, a pale glow as if I am being buried.

Food is light. Teeth are light. Her teeth grind back. Its
*Use* is her presence.

Her teeth are like a sling of teeth hitting you in the air.

So there are mother teeth and father teeth beginning from
the beginningless white and red *bindu*.

Now, in the *age of teeth*, I mean hers are swollen and I am
left with something I cannot piece together.

*White Bird*

*1*

A man wearing birds, *sitting* in birds, inside the birds' flow.
Together they're called *White Bird*.

*White Bird* grows tall. *White Bird* hugs his own legs back.
The meditation of sky streams into his heart so there's a
*passage of heart* into which he may relax.

*White Bird* relaxes back into his heart, breathing white, like
the beauty of a seed or wind in a bird's hair.

A man sits in wind wearing few clothes, but the birds
come and sit on him like clothes.

*White Bird* stops. Summer light swarms his shell and the blue shell breaks.

The beauty of his wing fills with sky.

A gull too drags its sky. As if it were an ear gathering in sky.

*Beauty is sky. Beauty is rain in sky's past sky.*

My mother's arm is pure, its curve of sky seeping into structures.

Then later someone says, *That person is a dead person.* So then I think, *The beauty of sky's color flows from her arm reminding me of her arm.*

*I want to <u>wear</u> sky,* I holler. (I am in tune with degrees of my mother hanging from death like a soft shoe.)

Her yellow armpit sags, like old newspapers would be lying fallow as they do on distant fields.

A man buys socks but it is really death lurking in sky. *I want to dust sky out so that my limbs swallow themselves.*

He looks, passing by death, as if he is new, *in sky now*, as he puts it.

*O look at the birds! They're combing each other's hair!* (He's watching a bird gather its gorgeousness.)

My mother is a line. Within the death-lines she is one. But a node on her blackens and then she is not my mother.

I know a bird whose color is sky before the sky admits itself. Like the brain of a color if sky admits the bird.

A mountain is visible *inside* the bird then. Its color dies then.

A queen bird releases into sky. *There's the sky!* someone says, as if there *is* sky, the *location* sky.

*That bird knows me well,* I'm thinking, because the bird is mostly dead.

*Here is a corner of sky,* mother says, fondling a dead bird wrapped up in her pocket. (The bird had lost sky. That's why it died.)

*I am the oscillations of a flower, <u>inside</u>, like a flower's brevity,* she whispers.

A tall bird tumbles through sky. The touch of its voice is like a raw egg folded into zero.

My mother feeds me air, the tablature of air, doubling air, forcing it to become air <u>to</u> something.

I dream of air (a box of air) because I conflate air with my dead mother. She could taste the flavor of the box and in her mind suck out the box. (Secretly she criticized people who didn't suck.)

Her feet swell in air. The ascending foot, like you could crawl inside the foot.

*Who is the end of my mother? Who is the end of my death?* (I am organizing myself backwards.)

*Flowers fall, but mountains blossom in air. Born in air, I'm in air already, like a broken piece of air.*

2

Sometimes a tree lies flat against sky and its outline in sky makes a sound.

The sound has a color that is not something I know.

*The sound of a flower goes anywhere,* you say. *The water of its breast dribbles down the grass, which is old grass, with old sound, barely any.*

So then I think, *My mother is dead but when I sleep with her, I'm old.*

A woman stands alone. She swings her eyes out past
nothing.

*If you look at a squirrel and see it very clearly, its feeling pulls
back, pulls its loyalty back.*

*Squirrels are always alone. May the squirrel never be alone,*
she continues, as if time were a bottle of water.

As if a young calf molts or a snake coils around a flower
and then *is* the flower.

*Is it true or false*, a child demands, hearing that petunia-lands exist.

For sound doesn't die, though its lineage may, like Buddha
Shakyamuni's dharma.

*Sharsin, Muni Sharsin*, they say. *Muni Sharsin* means Buddha
Shakyamuni's dharma, which the Buddha said, without the
lineage will die. Thus the longevity of a sound's *hand*
dissolves into its legacy of repertoire.

Which is *not* acquisitive, does *not* form a habit of being.
It's the loin of the habit of the sound.

*3*

*Can sand laugh?* You see sand and then sand's throat. I mean the lax throat of her death-rattle.

*Is it a whole throat? Be aware of the whole throat.*

Take the climate of her throat. Like she could set it on the sill and it would still be her throat.

Because things exist, and then exist, and their detritus is left in the mouth of the person.

I see a photograph of her throat, which is not the actual
throat. *Where is her throat in the wake of <u>that</u>?*
(I'm guessing *that* means *after* her throat.)

*Does it learn?* you ask. (I'm trying to remember if her
throat learned during its lifetime as my mother.)

Someone is the location of what *once was my mother*. (There
are pigs, dogs and someone is riding the dog.)

It's the still core of an eye, thus my mother *almost*. She begins in her
heart, like a step ladder of hearts all within one heart.

A little dog trapes across the edges of a carcass, its spots blowing toward birth.

The weight of its space creeps under space. (This is called 'opening the space gate.')

Her parakeet that died can release itself in space. (She pictures her mother in an agony of space, beyond what she can imagine as *being*, as if her mother *is*, somehow, without *being*.)

Take a maximum bird. One feather fills the canyon and its children eat plentifully. BECAUSE FROM TODAY SHE IS NOT DEAD.

# The Bardo Books

CONTENTS

*Death*

A man breaks fish. The man mentally smoothes its fins so that they don't stick out.

*I'm waiting to be black,* he's saying, but it is food he's uttering. I can see the food grow in his eyes.

Though the black diffusion of fish swims away from the horizon, the fish continue endlessly.

I *see* the fish who is my brother. Its time is pink like mine. We flow in the same yard.

Maybe my mother is a former fish whose throat
was broken by the man.

I offer her a word. I lift the word to the level of
my forehead.

*Where's my death?* she is asking. But I think it's the
clairvoyance of my mother, the instant in her
dream wandering around her body parts.

Once she saw sun draining down a mountain path,
like the ridges of a shell, the beauty of a hump on
death.

*Before my mother is dead*, I begin, but you say, *No.
'before' is a word.*

*Words <u>are</u> time. Of <u>is</u> its existence.*

The time of the word, *dead* (the word), hanging
from sky, is an activity that she knows from already
having been dead.

Time is not skin *in* which body parts are wrapped,
but *of* ineffable pink flamingo fluff, later, back in the
hotel room.

So there is this dream of a mother somewhere in death. Actually she isn't dead, but merely spaces I shuffle around.

As if a cold steel point is inserted in her with the sense that *this is correct, this is good to insert this inside you.*

*It's the dead person,* she thinks. Like a Harlem of *her* lying on either side of me, but someone says, *No! Go to school,* as if wherever she is *is* center but not the center *of* anything.

Then I go, *Oh, she's dead!* seeing as before, heavy rice-tassels ripening in the fields.

*

Low sun from above you on lilies, blue flags. She walks a hill and the cool sun is prescient she feels.

Like a garden of animals, caribou, birds, rhinoceros soaking, so that the sun emerges in them darkly.

*Dusk is like a hen absorbing herself into her chickens,* she murmurs.

The wrinkles of the sun swell on your back and I'm thinking, *There's the sun*, but it's just one of the five poisons.

A man stands on a hill. Light and birds and leaves
dribble from his fingers.

*Unnnnn,* he utters. *I am without rivers. I am without
a sound that can be replicated.*

As how light passes through death, like the skin of
a bird peeled from its wing.

A young bird honks, honk-honk-honk, as if its
feathers are a territory, too excavated, almost the
whole weather.

A body melts in sun. A herd melts. A melted herd is called *downward directness.*

Because what is isolated is stopped. Air's *inside* is caught. *Upward directness* stopped is like movement's absolute inside.

A hat might exist, in this sun, like snow in sun or a flower pressing sun.

*The beauty of the hat is because our world is situated at the heart level of Buddha Immense Ocean Vairochana,* a person remarks.

Sun slips to sea as if air were sea so that within slipping there is existence.

Sea is fact. And each sea avuncular like a family structure.

I look out to sea and the green ripples wave and a little boat drifts like a concept I can forget about.

The splendor of water admits a line of morning light, which could be light repelling its own limit or light irrespective of her sense of limit.

Somehow a bird slips away from its limits,
therefore it exists, like a rainbow or a raindrop.

The fusion of a shell touches a current of shells, or
like the inside of a wave, if I died, it would be the
same as seeing the wave in a mirror.

If I look at the sun, slowly, imagining it's a
meadowlark, something is solidified in the tense
mind of my hand.

A mirror *appears* to take my hand inside, but I
want my hand to be its own inside.

Which is *of* time, like being *fed* time. Taste is in her neck, the city of her body.

A dead boy leaves a trail in a house toward the bottom of its body.

Like if a peach dies and becomes decipherable, like the inside of my food.

Daylight in a voice or the skin of sea is a separate gesture cordoned off as if for *that* you would have to stand in line.

I am now a person touched by sea, the motion of sea inside the horse, harvesting the horse.

*Maybe the artist drew the horse's shell <u>after</u> it was a horse.*

*The beauty of a horse is forever,* you mutter. *The scale of a horse inside a man or a man possessed by a dzo pulling a blazing cart of fire—the lines of thought cannot, like a 'shippei,' be grasped tightly in one's fist.*

*If a horse eats sea, it's sea's endless rocking land, the climax of one becoming one again, recycling what has never left.*

*Bathing Suit*

A woman begins, is the value of space, like a child
in a pool, shuffling air in which hard wood is air.

She breathes through wood, taking sharp quick
breaths. *I want the soft cloth of children*, she's saying.

Her breath has height and the texture of children
swimming, new swim, out and out, yet clearly
touching the bottom. *The mind of wood may rest
itself to completion*, she murmurs.

Wood and air is swimming there, in the space of
air filtered through a dark forgotten memory.

She is complete air. She tucks herself in air, as in the taste of breath, the babysteps of breath.

She is anterior to her air and tries to tie air like a ball.

Someone gives me a ball and I tie up the ball. I feel certain that I want to tie the ball.

She calls it air because it's there like air, but actually it's a kind of stupidity.

Swimming is like a captivity in its body. Every minute in a row I am swimming everywhere and wanting to spend my time swimming swimming swimming.

Because death, too, is an integer. I say 'grass' and it follows me into longevity.

The absence of time, like grass without time, or a lizard in its skin but outside time so that its purity lay in its body.

The brain of the sky snaps an instant to its purity because everything perceived is Buddha Vairochana.

My mind vanishes then. Inside its skin it has its
male and female aspects.

A pool of mind is a passage of light, raw light, the
membrane between the watery part of light.

A person flows through wood and is the breath of
a swimmer, like two dead people in love.

Air in a heart is the same air resting there.

*

A woman walks but she is dead. Her red dress is dead. She is pasted on a page like a paper doll.

There is a handbag and hat that can be separately attached, which is how clothing exists if the person is not living.

She longs for herself in the stray black bonnet, alone, by the sea, soft as a wave.

She takes in sky like a flower sky. *If I see you, then see you as if you were an outline, it's like seeing an avoidance.*

An image of a body has the sweet porous colors of
body + ideal body, like the image of a bather
standing under sky where sky, a haze of pink,
traces itself onto the person's body.

Piercing a bather snuggly wrapped in towel,
piercing straight through her body.

To be a small body on the underside of the color. *A
housekeeper of color*, someone remarks. (A bird
swims in time that has already escaped.)

I see the bather's legs, long and clipped, its posture
of mind rooting repetitious shadows.

The body is a uniform wearing the person. Color leaks out. A painted bather's body is how light looks like this color.

A bather's cap and suit mark that person. Blue is the form of the feeling of her standing within boards shaped like a skeleton of sky.

Boards in sky have a plethora of sky as if it's sky that's being constructed.

The mark is interior, like the film of an angel disengaging from its body, wrapping itself around a life, saying *I am my own angel.*

Opaque light under a bather's knee, reflecting from its knee, because we're through the knee, seeing a miasma of lustrous color.

As if sky *is* knee because of the bather and sky's proximity.

A bardo of knee makes time that is a color. (The interval of a knee where red skips to a color.)

So a painter paints a shape that is an appearance of time's color, like a word appears as object and can *be* the object even in darkened space.

Sky sheds words. The language of its space
harkens toward direction, as if each object has its
indigenous essential direction and the painter paints
*that.*

The interest in a knee wells up from light, like time
plucked from myriad pools of time that whisper, *I
am that time.*

Roses are pure gold, their presence sartorial,
upright. Scent is cast by their shadow.

I sleep myself back to a set point of sky, like a *ration
of sky,* raising the *mass of doubt.*

*Black*

A black bird's hair flows in the wind as if instinct pursues forward but forward is inside its body.

Because ordinary birds cannot implant as an animating principle the non-direction of breath.

A black bird lifts. Direction, not sensed, but *being* in the time of the bird's body which the *is-ness* of its nest matches.

*I know your breath.* The vibration *now* channels through the black part because black-on-black is how its breath is sheltered.

Sweet water on the bird (the bounteous color of black as a form) dissolves back into its body.

High black, like butterflies leaving imprints, in deference to that, which, after disappearance, is what is left.

The allure is time, direction underneath itself, falling through wind, gushing through a mountain stream.

She stares into a lake. A butterfly drifts on the surface of the water. Its wing is torn and she imagines its life rising briefly above its death before drifting off.

A body dissolves and there is no memory of its having been undissolving.

Like a bird whose hair got swallowed of its color. It is sizeless, jigsawing red, as if red is the surrogate of all possible places.

A man taps a bird on the window of its head. *He can dissolve without passing away,* someone says.

*Then* I am in my body but not captive in my body, because the reflection of my body as a "high" black bird got swallowed up.

I describe an ideal of bird, a content of mind, like the sharpening of her hair so that she has little *vajras* of hair. *Don't suck your hair,* her mother yells.

An ideal of something ripening, a child's bird near a nobleman's. *I want to put my bird near his so it will learn to sing with the same beautiful voice,* the child explains.

Her body has a sound and each limb I trace around my leg. Its breath-imprints paint the space of breath-swept thought.

Like crammed flowers in a barrel hold together the heart of the person.

*Vajra* is extent, *no hair* the space of being so happy. A mother abides and is in favor of her (as at a baseball game sort of).

A wind-stroke of abiding, like the earth on its axis, which as we find out, doesn't make any difference.

To cultivate the awkward eye, the bird's back eye, under its shoulder sleeping (in the bottom way of a being's shrill sleep).

The circumference of her sleep makes a limit in her body so that she cannot move beyond the elusive space of her body.

The *no-hair* of her is exact her, so the mother thinks, *I am <u>not</u> her.*

Then the mother fights. *I <u>am</u> her also. Somewhere, like the bird, is why I keep one near me also.*

*Slow* words are on its belly. If you crawl under the bird, you see script you can decipher.

A lexicon of hair (like a ballet of hair) so that repeatedly we converge on the edge of earth.

*Cow*

A woman paints cows in the passionate arena of some easiness in her.

She relaxes into cow and paints a full and complete rectangle of color from her own memory.

Like a wheelbarrow of cow (red squares may faintly vary according to the grass, which the woman doesn't paint).

The woman paints cows but she is actually painting her mind waving a *khata* for three seconds at death.

Of course there is the painting of a blue girl as if the artist's mother were dead.

*I too am in deadland.* That quickening sense, as if she were a hall. The animals of a person come out.

Once I was pure. Now the casing of kittens unfolds on my bed and my mother's ignorance spills out.

If she cooks I am afraid. If she hears I'm in the dynasty.

Then a bird swoops down, soaring like a vulture.
The tail of the bird shines its domino
white/red/black.

No-cow is cow, cow-time, or the fun of its calf,
who is ticklish and laughs.

So there's a *double* cow, my dead mother's mind,
instead of her having her own.

A woman *plans* her mind but quickly pastes
something over it so it is lost.

The milk-white bird lands on a cow's head. The coils of the bird are like the *value* of wind suddenly.

The cow sits without breath, skin colored like a tree.

The moon could be a boat and the cow jumps over the boat only it is sitting and breathless and there is no water.

An old cow moos from below itself upwards. In the gaps of the cow, because the light of the moon makes the cow REAL.

A brown and white cow grazes on a hill. A
common cow merging with the hill, as if it were a
shelf holding all of the hill's karma.

The speed of the hill slows. *Its eyes are just
beginning,* you proffer.

A dead person becomes permeable. *I'm that
buttercup! I'm golden in the cow, a clear gold
buttercup blossoming in the cow's stomach.*

The tenderness of rushes and sweet voice of birds,
a broom and bell till all sounds fluff them out.

*Hunt*

A songbird steps through sky, absorbs the moor
into its shadows. Its woolly bottom carries the
number of nights it has been alive.

The habit of sky moves in its bones. As how a
verb, energetically transcends its sphere of
meaning. The *chore* of it is the meaning.

The movement of the land, wet and cold, rubs the
man's limbs. His gun is slack like an intelligence he
can't quite muster.

A game bird's flesh in air absorbs the brother air of
his body. As if the bird is hunting his body and
*knows* the use of his body.

The head of a bird glows. Is it day or the bird?
(The motility of its edges seeps through day like
water.)

Pieces of day. A pigeon moves in its body. *If you
leave air, there is no air,* someone says.

Sky bathes air like lineage brought from air. *I have
a pearl between my tail which can't cross over the
threshold.*

The wing of the bird drains of its flight as if one's
life is sped up so one can die.

The beauty of a kill hangs in fog, which is what the
man is seeking. He is married to kill still living
there.

He is in and out of color. Like he could *pet* the
color, whose correlate is nativity.

*My stumps have knees but my legs cannot hold them.*
(Plum light weaves through my idea of the sky's
body.)

A bird is brush, its gaze a throb. Its blueblack
wings dip and slip.

It feels like decomposition, flesh, rare-pink, a nick
in the bird's wing.

The hair of the bird, digested by its mind in the
mind of its karmic murderer.

Whose bardo may be shot up. I *eat* sky, then the
outcome of its body. (The belly of the bird
waddles through flowers.)

As if he eats his former mind thus twice-killing the
bird and the potential of the bird. A moor fowl in
the tentative sense of *locale*.

*Birth*

You are pock-marked like my birth. The wrongdoing of one in a long stream of Indian nobles.

As if calamity rode in and no one was there. A war of one or no war being so violent.

Like the Church or war-torn hearts afterwards in the alley, the animal's eyes, dust to what is feral.

The press of them, like cups, which is the smell of my birth in them.

You come like a gust and intimately, where *intimate*
is my finger.

Touching you, inside a stone, in the hearth of a
house there.

Your mind is alluvial. If you roam I see the stubble
of water pierce through you like an arrow.

A bird hums inside its beauty like the inside of a
sound heard only by its bird.

If a bird arises from time and then the quick shape
of something yellow, its gorgeousness is there.

A tin of snow is your gift. The idea of immanence,
a decoy of a time.

The idea moves into other bodies. Cage-birds
chirp in the bedroom of a sick person, making their
singing esoteric.

I *count* snow as if one, two, three *live* in the snow,
are part of the snow's paradisical logic.

# Figures in Blue

CONTENTS

## DAFFODILS

A woman alone at a large open window gazes at
the sky. The soft flesh of her arm folds around a
basket. If she is dead, the colors may be alive.

Her soft flesh holds a premonition of her, calls its
form within the form of its space in sky.

She is miming sky with her body. *Taming* its color,
like a double her of color.

There is a sense of intense activity in the buildings
and neighborhood, so familiar, yet her skin is not
that.

Angst from the street, but what prevails is the face
of a person waiting.

An agony of light chugs through her body.

If she could roll out her body, like make a road of
her body, there is the sense of that being all there is.

As if her flesh were a habit, a woman stands in sky,
catching it in the drape of her dress.

As she rests in the bare window she is dead. *I (am dead)* she says. It stands like a point of view.

A strip of death is on the woman's arm.

She wants the death eagerly, like time tucked in her arm. *On the crest you can just touch death,* she feels.

She sees an arm (the boundless ordinary nature of her arm) in a gown, in the sky, wrapped in a column of the unsaid.

Sky like sea, around a woman hugged by sea.

A man is a response (like sky and a sea wall). The *float* of him sinks, then appears on the horizon.

*I am exempt from sky if I empty myself toward it.* The flaccid man's ribs absorb the thick musculature of her arm.

Daffodils range, placated by time, but it is the habit of deep slumber.

EAGLE

An old man sits, quiet like a log. His knees are
crossed. Somehow he is stalling, unplaced, like the
woods of his head.

If he sees age, it is good age he feels.

As if time happens twice in the crux of his body.
But it waits.

The spine of an animal coils in air as it dangles from
a limb, sun stroking it nervously.

The man sees blue in a bulbous core of light. His
outline bobs just outside his body.

There are animals in his body (the knowing of what
locomotes the folds of a man's body).

Sun spalls time. Something is heard but he is dead.
*Giddy* describes the animal climbing out of his eyes.

As the animal creeps away, a
rising eagle empties (gathers slowly) into his body.

The eventual empty sky or incremental bardos of sky, as if sky is one continuous living membrane.

The ridge of the eagle's motility in my mind dwarfs its vanishing in clouds.

I *think* I see the contour of its movement (the bird's flying outside the possibilities of its body). It leans into the land, then drains into sky.

As if a boundary included in its disappearance also imprints the bird, sky and the part of sky that's thought.

I dream myself to being the majesty of a body, a sphere with an eye as in the self-view of a mental body.

I dream myself to a shape that looks like a fresh smell.

The sloppiness of birth, if I seek its tail in the crack of myself, whose poison, excrescence, great gelatinous spookiness hang like an old breast on the person.

The androgynous bearing of a breast, sagging in day like a normal breast, the normal day of *no-day*, as if she were a fog leaning over and asking a question.

SPRING

A child peers from the spines of a sapling, tender
like soft eyes. A knuckle propping her cheek seems
stiff, awkwardly awake in a dark rivet of sun.

Now is *between* joining what is present to one.

Light on the blue wall is making the child public,
though she is alone, miscible, her feet are alone.

To replay time, like a child's favorite story, has the
same soothing sense (her being a rabbit) again.

The foreclosure of a life being locked into this sky, this orb of seasons and death, such as the spring of sky.

If a baby walks in sky, she too is an example of how containers simply amplify karmic structure.

Pink flesh makes a covenant. An eye is silk and slips out.

The play of a person's face, in perfect precision with her, drifts in sky like a boat.

Like she might trip over her body wandering through a scarlet field. If the container formulates from inside, slippage becomes hostile.

Spring touches the nonlocation of her ground, the pace of her mind as a shield.

There is a string around a mind still *situated* in her body though no longer biologically *seated* in her body.

Many insects collect there. It is a grieving ground.

Sometimes the sky looks like ducks and I remember
floating on an arrow toward a city.

Like time in a foot where sky is the foot. A
thinking person's thoughts die in little clumps.

So the impact of the arrow, the *brain* of the arrow.

When it dies its bones and tongue smell of spring as
if spring were something *made* in its body and later
revealed by its body.

JUKE BOX

A woman in her doorway looks up. She raises her
hand to her hat as her head tilts back. Summer is
high. The image of sun fusing with her body such
that she *becomes* the sun, its place in sky resting
back toward herself watching.

Her feet are bare in high-heeled shoes. Soft folds
of her dress stir in a slight breeze.

The description is a protection, a barrier placed as
a scene. There is tension between herself and the
scene.

The brim of her hat dips. Its motion is time.
There is tension between the time of her hat's
dipping and the time of the sun streaming through
sky, creating decrepitation in her body.

The woman is loose. Her bones move as she rests back on her lungs. The woman breathes in conjunction with her lungs as if everything in her world were contained within a bagpipe.

Her body no longer shields her, she feels. She lowers her arm and brushes its skin to remove the tension that has resulted.

It is a thick body, like tea leaves or lamb. A body like sweet fruit.

She leans against a piano. Her body is not a pianist's though.

A woman hungering for her body moves along the edges of her body. She moves it to her heart, toward the belly of its hair.

The chaos in a hair, a flank of hair, but the true flank refuses to spread farther than its own body.

Sound cuts space bleeding in her bones, tourniquets of sound in her hemline.

Being the grandmother of her sound, the great great grandmother of her highest lightest sound, like an unsound, sound with a backbone.

A moth spreads funerary wings across a fragment
of sky. I see her skin (the *sound* in skin) hovering in
its body.

Dusk over grass lights a spot on the moth's wing.

There is a dance in her, but she will not know it.
She looks away because she sees this.

A juke box dissolves, calms into a shuffle, a slow
dance of days in which she can be ready.

FUZZ

If you look you see a little fuzz of hair above the
head and neck of a blonde woman. She appears to
be standing, waiting in a stall, reading a magazine.

Her headband clears a space that she inhabits if I
think of her.

What is the real face? The photograph of someone
living, but it is a paper face, double non-living.

*Is how we wait for our mind to know what we are,* the
fragrance of a number gone.

I want to cry when I see her hair, stiff with an idea
of a place she might take up.

Her skirt is loosely feral. Gravity is a lesion on her.

Her laugh I infer from the hair. *I live in my hair,* she
says to you casually, like a caucus of hair
opprobriously abusing its own hair.

She will relax and be her hair, the spine of each
hair. Little hairs on your forearm.

Sky gathers around her hair. She lifts her hand.
Sky crawls under her hand as if it recognizes its
mother.

Her hand *is and always will be* the life inside a hand.
The belly of the hand is in the woman's eyes.

Time is umbilical, as if her hand suddenly defines *my*
amount, more accurately than my amount.

A cop's black leather hand pushes back night
because he knows he can. (He is a shepherd of
fire.)

She passes herself (and her periphery) walking
*down* as if *down* were handcuffing her.

All arrows point down. Night abides making space
for its light because night recognizes its same light
family.

There is a robbery. The lapse of a person (the
mulling of its eye) whirring in air a few centimeters
off.

Night rubs night so that *death can carry the sky to
the people.*

## SPRIG OF LAUREL

A woman's full body in the folds of her soft full
body may be a portrait of death.

She is looking at sky, loosely alive. The painter
paints light so that its breath is exposed in the folds
of her t-shirt against her shoulder.

Her hair is loose, pushed back behind her hand. It
bends *in* like a child.

May I loosely let go of her emaciated hand, like a
turkey in flight hangs in sky, loosely falling away
from its flying.

That the painter requires a sprig confuses her. He sticks the sprig into her hand. *The gnarled causes of a hand are beginningless,* she's thinking.

Air seeks the awareness of her, making a thin film between life.

Soft desolation keeps churning against a wall. *If I carry my shell up, the image of a bird. Hell is a bird which flickers in and out of being married like that.*

The room exists partially to mimic a bird flowing, but it leaves a bad color.

The wait of a woman at the edge of air, sweetly
like a wing, swift and awake, so as to sweep the air
close in.

An image of her heart is showing on its face, which
turns inside out so that the heart is holding the
face.

She smiles the smile of the face as it has appeared
both during its growing and later during its
samadhi. Even angels have faces in her, she feels.

*Until* is the memory of one—*until-when grasses*—or
*how-long grasses* is her own memory of one.

*Is there, without the girl, a girl holding a sprig?* (I'm
wondering if she is simply an old longing.)

Like if you die but you don't, does your feeling for
the girl disappear?

If air dies but the girl is living, what happens to my
feeling if she is Vajrapani?

I offer light and smoke to an unassailable space, an
aphasia of space, like a *belt* of space.

## TULIP

A woman sits facing light. Sun hits her hands
resting on a flowered dress. A long row of
windows stand in the dawn quietly.

So that we too (*that's* our mind). She is not
existing in sitting's aspect.

We don't see her eyes. We *infer* that she is
reading from the texture of her skin. As if her skin
is reading.

To which her body, she feels, is surrogate. The
space is there but not available, which the act of
reading addresses.

The resonance of a reader's mind coagulates in her earth sign. Earth is time, then making a little bowl of it for her head.

As if time were skin, like a family of her body,

*I want the boy erect,* she says. *I want him like a card as its colors fold around it.* She sees the color of the dead one so that she could be dead again.

Autumn is the frame. Red leaves, violet sky, like a chop signing him off.

Sometimes I hear her death, like lip from behind a word. Words are a prick, *prick, prick,* thin as air, but some say. *No! She's round like a ball.*

The word is alive. I speak it by touch. *My eyes bulge and my mouth puckers, but I am dead first,* she is saying.

The lip moves sleepily. In sticky summer like a heavy foot. *See, it's wandering through a vibrant field of flowers!*

No one arrives, which has the pleasant feeling of continuous sky.

A moth breaks off sky. It spins around then lands
on a blue wall. A marking on its wing trails through
its fur.

Wind through a hill *because* of the hill holding a
place for it, is how it can be that.

*Its feathers are broken.* Whose long arc of pastness,
like the wings of a crane fanning out in space.

Death is imposed on blowing branches against a
wall, like nearness and life, beauty and wilting tulips.

TREE

A girl lolls on grass in a tutu. *The blue ruffle of a violet is the same as sky,* she's thinking. (Blue is not a location but a warmth of pressure around an object.)

Gathering rain presses against sky, then falls in squares mirroring the farmland.

Tonally it is dark. The musicality of a land (almost *neon* in the palm) plays a doubly dark magnetic field.

The *thought* of sky, dispersing itself to its own full origin, may be death in its still quiet flush.

*I am older from sky, such as a waltz dovetailing sky.* A guardian of sky sprinkles saffron across her body.

Appearance quells in patterns against light, the curve of her hip, then flaring and draping over something we can't see.

If she could rest in sky, but she is aggravated. A tuft of cotton sticks out from an ear.

A fundament of time is exactly a cigarette, the vagaries of a thumb suddenly weak and drifting.

The dissepiment may be a tree. Roots are bones,
bone to bone in strange woolly clusters.

The corpse is alive though. Its tongue is its mind as
soon as it wakes up.

Mountains of sad trees but one tree lays its limbs
out wide, direction carpeled to a simple fruit.

A caravan of heads, rolls and rolls of swaddled
heads, fades into a bluebird's call.

Rain through sky, through the greenery of sky. Fire
and rain create a pocket.

You are dead. Something in the pocket reaches for
you. The spirit just sticks its hand into your body.

Then he gives it back. *A golden carp of golden bones
escapes you,* it says.

The ache of a tree, like an arabesque of bones,
sheds its trace imperceptibly.

THUMB

A woman partially hidden by a wall stands in
midday light. She is a rounded person with soft
brown skin. A curl falls on her forehead.

The fullness of the setting demands a potential
connected object so that the image of her doesn't
fragment.

A second woman seated facing away eludes space
by an unseen motion, the peep of her hat, the
beauty of thin leaves layering sky onto the woman
standing.

Wings of sky make flowers that look like birds, a
spire of delicacy inside the person.

The view of a partially hidden woman is absolutely alive. Someone is jealous. A man shuffles by if he is alone.

How light hits air is how the weight of her appearance, a tulip feathering out, a painter paints *that,* the feather-weight of appearance carried by a woman's body.

A town of women grow in light. If she's free. (A dab of blue is not freedom though.)

The man wears blue but he has not achieved the purity of blue. What is not blue's purity is like another person.

I am watching sky and a dark man watching sky.
The time of this sky is the non-time of looking.

A vast amount of sky may take place inside his
belly. If he sneezes it is there like his own twin
body.

Part of sky is a clear line of intensity but part
scatters like sun over a pool.

In the lordosis of sky the pulse of his blazing white
undershirt refracts such that light stops *behind* itself
inside his belly button.

A person waits. A brown bare body holds the
tension of waiting. Nothing moves except (slightly)
his thumb resting on the waist of his jeans.

The excursion is in the neck, like sky along his
neck. As how the eyes of a bird to a person from
a distance form an intimacy one can't touch.

I make pleasant. If he waits for the portion he will
ultimately be, like shine in a deep pool or wind in
a rabbit's eyes. I place my heart in some wishbone
there.

The wishbone pops like time in the dead man.

BLACK

A humpback wearing red fishes in black water. He
leans against a tree if it is angled in a cloudless
morning.

A bird flies out. Pierced hair slithers onto its wing.

I am startled by the parity of a simple action by a
simple person relatively relaxed, covered by time.

The size of time works through day, like fish
breathing mud, squirming against day's barriers.

Perhaps the artist, as an effigy of death, makes the bird to avoid or ward death off. The bird could be suicide (or way of performing a natural process).

Since the wakening of the bird, correlates (empty of the bird) may look like a higher stage of bird.

Mountains and rivers are faces with hollow eyes. Stilettos in air hang prettily from blue satin.

Clouds are like a string of pearls where one pearl is black and that's why they're all there.

A cloud in the shape of a bird hangs low in evening sky. Its shadow forms a hump.

The cloud could be a door swiveling in space, a spark of lavender in grass, only it is black.

*If black peers from the death of me, I may lose track of its trajectory, confusing it with life, thinking it is my life.*

A nerve of sky pierces my side so I walk with a limp, which reminds me of a mountain's breast.

A painter paints a mountain, *shedding* the mountain.
(Black replaces black in the subtle crevice between
himself and what he discards.)

If he is where someone lives then. *We place ribbons
on our mountain and let its water fall out.*

You can kill a mountain by shutting your eyes or
looking at the mountain thinking of your dead
mother.

No color rises. Orange turns to sand in a country
without flowers.

## COW

If you throw some earth on a table, the figures in the earth, what is there to be derived, from air, from a spell, like a flavor.

There is a geomancy *there,* taken from the harbor.

Immanence in eating, what stands in front of it, so that when something happens, it has already happened also.

*Also* is time. An eater places that against a numerology of color, like the brown wall of the room, which is neither earth nor his dark hand.

The thought in a wrist and each bare lobe of hand.
Yellow is crucial in the gentle unfolding of its earth
element.

Hunger is the border, divination the table, a
context clean of all past expression.

I am born each minute that the man eats bread. I
place a palm against his brow. My mind is what he
digests.

If I think of the person, yellow almost *becomes* the
person because my mind and the thing don't
separate.

An eating man's neck, free of all justification in him, is a portrait of time swallowing a neck. Electrical swallowing speaks the ache of time in his chewing.

I'm reminded of a dog, knocking over cans, scarfing.

A neck is a mental neck and the throat swallowing death thinks that it is still lunching.

*A petunia taking birth near a cow means that the teller (time) will definitely complete the yugas,* it rambles.

A cow wearing red is gliding toward rebirth. Its mind is a plum that it sucks while they tear up its body.

He draws the cow down into his body so it can rest and finally sleep within his body.

Like if snow were food, the sense of miles and miles of snow. Still, the person's throat has not even a particle of snow in it.

If snow were crafted in earth with it in mind instead of sourcing it from sky (like the pair of lovers floating in sky with death in mind).

## MEADOW

A face in the light of you, which is dusk or early morning. Wind in hay and the tall anchoring of a blanket, as if her hair were the blanket.

A cat bays in the moon whose face appears in the light of you.

Dew is thick. The loosening of its weight holds an even placement of view.

Arms and hair curve like grass in the exact amount of their sleeves.

Acres of red born in the same sky. A man watches
light stretch and thin across the hay bundles.

To comb a flame, his face against her hair. Aghast
is what abides beyond the scope of shape.

Shape is space in its aspect of brilliance, her face
through shifting breeze brushing hair over shadows.

The *waist* of a scene expands beyond its boundaries
so that meadow convexes anterior to sky, like a
bulge in sky, as if it were dead.

The eye of the painter focusing on a meadow is how my mind wants the space of its real dead body.

They want it to be kinship, *we two together,* but in fact it is a splurge of shape (the potential shape of sky).

Someone paints night, space consecutive with darkness, as if one space is *more* dead.

Death is space whose appearance results from space, unbridled in the soft of *low,* emergent face on stone.

Night releases to *I* as an object. A winterland of limbs. (The winter of her body *is* this very body dead.)

As if sky were alone a century beforehand. The sound, heavy through night, retains its weight in light.

I locate you back to the outreaches of sky. Low slow land is a transparency in her body.

Prehistoric quiet covers up day like a sheet.

# *The Twelve* Nidānas

NOTE

*Nidāna* (Pali/Sanskrit): "cause, foundation, source, origin."
The twelve *nidānas* are an application of the Buddhist
concept of dependent origination. They identify the origin
of suffering to be ignorance.

I

A man's hand in the midst of him, a simple
expression of earth, the junction of red earth in
lieu of something indeterminable in the person.

The anthem of his hand, the flesh of his dark hand,
as in the blood of someone you know.

The attention of a leaf presses itself outwards.
How many lights pierce through the clouds
achieving themselves in its bit of space.

A tattoo of leaves touches his head lightly, like an
angel's hand anointing his crown, passing on the
light of him.

A man may be carrying the images of an angel's body, the division of light being the tilt of an angel's body.

He is wanting the complete light, the sense of arising trapped in the angel's body.

A concentration toward okay between what is presented to one, some subtlety coming to one.

Like an absence that one carries, light vanishes light, innocuous space beyond what one recalls.

The shadows of two people make a darkness in a field indistinguishable from the two people.

As how a silhouette of space, imaging the angel's dark form, as if his hand in pledge behind the eyesocket were internalized.

His image of him, whether his angel is dark, a dark dark angel as a transparency on his desire.

A filigree of space tips alluringly upwards as if it were imaging his own guts and belly.

Maybe he were a queen then. Maybe so many queens in a reality that is fed queens.

The city is an outbreath, a dark fabric of sky, as if sky were the angel's eyes.

A cat gets up, walks slowly over to sky, intuiting a sky that simply dissolves into a cat's body.

In the congregate of moving, dawn dissolves to sky, what holds between his feeling and a cityscape of sky.

II

The sky bleeds dark and lucent from its writing. A
calf is clearly struggling.

The absorption of a star, a linguistic signal, allows
the sky to dangle there.

Elements are like memory and function as a
support. Earth is easy, though it moves to the
ground and vanishes.

Her mind pours light on a stalk-still bird and it *stays*
still, then moves to the ground and vanishes.

Something in the calf holds hostage as a fight, like war in its family that has descended in its body.

She *sees* calf, the procession of a body. It is a baby engrossed in a footprint so its head is down.

Leaving one guessing. *Is this real? Is this a fact?* Repetition is and is part of the calf. (I am feeling its feeling deep in my armpit.)

Repetitive, *not* an irreducible spacing, is easily closed off, like dreaming or forgetting that in fact you *are* a calf.

If she promises to be her eyes, the extension into space, not the calf but the contiguous motion of its body.

Because the partial mind of seeing (the invisible-inclusive eye) binds what's unavailable to what you see.

Touch without touch, action without action. a feather-light eye touches the world back, like her death or above zero (if she were a lamb climbing out of her eyes).

I seal space, closing my eyes lightly, touching things lightly, because my eyes touch and are touched and this has become onerous.

What if seeing and touching were not
simultaneous, that having seen, the product of your
seeing does not come back to you?

If time boycotts time *and* falls to clear seeing, its
ersatz life exposed?

Pairs of eyes peer through the dark, not seeing
*something* but just the consciousness, *knowing*
knowing seeing.

Like you could skip seeing and just *be* seeing
because the past of an eye comes from
everywhere.

III

I walk through trees, a series of squat willows, and
see the space between the willows as time.

Because it's not the space, it's the emptiness of
mind (whose energy is grounded to its darkest
possible color).

Taking birth beneath a tree, I want to feel my
longing for the tree, my deep thought of you in its
disentangled precision of stillness.

One bends, taking its time, a full earth of time.
*How do I wander into its leaf?*

Merely touching earth, gently touching the awareness of earth, like the beginning of day in earth.

Leaves stretch to sun, the full breath of sun, but I am left gasping.

My reference point is fading. The underleaf is blank. But blank itself catches me in a kind of double-take.

A gap exists but she refuses to see it, which is a third sort of fuging, like the darkly yellow on the leaf's bottom.

*That* yellow cala lily, earth and earth-consecutive-with-darkness, a coincidence of blood and dark and color, *such a yellow*, heavy and unknown.

Indexed to light, this card of light folds around the sleeve of your body.

We take shelter in abyss, which looks like a color, magenta calligraphed in a cala lily's cup, deep in the cup, its fire.

Color filters light is not the net color that the cala lily *tells* by way of its earth sign.

IV

Night is her skin, its pleats the quiet fold of her.
Background and foreground are the memory of a
skin wearing dynasties of her.

A bird touches night and her skin moves as if it
were tied to this.

As if a mass accumulates in a narrative of space.
*Now* preserves as a robin opening out of its
capacity in me.

I want to pet it. I want to cry. The intimacy of a
word *before* it is a word, so that it's *now*, in the
interval, wears its own full body.

How many tiers live in a word and the hues of the
tiers in the space of the word's awareness.

*I*, the word, in the space of my form, imaging my
form, like a lion in its death throes.

*I swallow you* and *emergence in a word.* (The word's
shape is how death looks like this image.)

A cold press of wind through a word's tired body
could be hell or a word separate from its word.

To feel into a word, which may be neutral, but may
be like an animal who *gets* the word, as if the word
were a *lesion* in its body.

The lesion could be freedom because a word has
no location, like a break in the hills. (Mostly our
words are skeletons of themselves.)

One senses the transparent quality of its body, an
unchangeable power that runs alongside its body.

I am a word. I am the ultimate fearless word,
beauty or sky so that there is nothing in the way.

A word lands on her cheeks. *Unspeakable* is the word. *Unspeakable* is the crutch, the *cane* of the word, the transparency of the word that relates to her as a body.

As how several letters cast a sense of time, like a painting casts depth, which is the image of death in a room.

Then the dream of the word amalgamates. First there's sky, then the full comportment of a body. Sky-swaddled words catch the light of death.

I want to believe each word, like pray to the word, because you want to believe in its denial, forgiveness, everything.

A word lay in snow. If you lift the snow and
suspend your idea of the possible, it's like space
linking space to all constellations of that word.

The sheer resplendence of a word, as how the
daughter of a word, a whole lineage pouring out
from its god-father.

A child picks up a word. It's the enjoyment of the
word, the shape of all commodious expressions
that the mind living in that word carries.

In a tapestry of texts, I am in the moment of one,
as if I had gone to sleep.

V

I juxtapose pink with weather, seeing color emerge
from shape. Pink constellates to a pig's body.

Pink's trajectory, inclusive of pig, breeds pink into a
legacy, but the real pink transmits its pinkness to
the pig.

The pig looks pink because it's lost track of the
*possibility* of being made vivid. (*A rose is a rose is a
rose* brilliantly demonstrates the part of a rose
that's impossible.)

It burns a background to itself. A tenderness
comes out. *That's* the leap, the already-known, like
a rose seed.

Yes is a style. I grow an extra bone. *Here is my bone*, which makes me happy.

Its yes is and always has existed.

But if I misuse it, if now, seeing my bone, I make use of it in a negative sense, which is vivid, even shocking because I carry my own style in them.

You are involved with a style of being, relating your experience with a perception of your experience, e.g., crazy-shell pink, but pink reduces itself to nothing.

I am a limb braced on a trapeze, but I am an ostrich dreaming with my eyes shut.

If the pink is "swimmy" (it almost makes me cry—I could dwell on something that could happen).

The forefather of a dream may be jealous and hoard the dream. (I am again that bird, rosy plumage taut, ribs holding my scrawny body, which is an extremely crowded situation.)

What swims around the dream comes back. Me and my projections are put into a bag and I push as hard as I can.

I am trying to fit into one particular bag, which
becomes my limbs, a confabulation of infinity.

Essence doesn't flee. Essence stays with being.
Time puffs itself into a thing, like saturation, which
can resemble a pink color.

As how the consumption of time will alleviate
time's stoppage to the degree that the person *feels*
time's stoppage.

*How* is style, toggling illusory and dream, instead of
coming across the material of a dream, offering it
space because terror needs space.

VI

A teller's face recedes. Silver bars entrap his
shoulder, tie and shirt collar. If you search for his face,
but it's the *no-search* that finds his face.

*How much does it cost to find his face?* (Now I am a
slim finder of his face.)

He passes me money. His hand does not touch the
bills that I receive because relinquishing receiving, I
just take the money.

The transaction questions presence. If I arrive on
both sides of receiving, everything disappears.

One face of *no* face moving casually like a normal face. (Though the man is naked, his face seems even more naked.)

Because energy needs a context of definite, specific events. *If you are handless, there is still the environment of hands, like a throat of hands about to swallow your body.*

His shirtsleeve is hiked exposing a man's wrist, vulnerable, droopy, as if the man's energy floods into his hand, skipping the wrist, which could be the wrist of a different man.

The flesh is white. Cold light yields a sting of hours, time defined, no long upright.

The essence of its white is like a king wearing a
hand. (That the king is wearing a hand depends on
the viewpoint of the person.)

A symbol of white spreads across the palm, a
legacy of wind, like air that is yours.

Something begins, is loosely held in one's body,
casting a sense of depth (as if its symbol *is* one's
body).

A glove on my cupped hand cradles my lung,
anchoring to the extreme, up and up to the hand
that is so extreme.

It's how image and matter falter. Mother and child meet but the mother's mind does not meet.

You can see this in her hand, ring finger lax, then the laxing itself takes on existence.

First sky, the fatty mound of a thumb, then figures topped by shapes inferred to have existence because sky undeniably has existence.

A person's hand is how sky looks like this body, which is so sad but is not her hand.

VII

A woman's mind is young. It kneels like a child at
bedtime. At the breathline of her wash she makes
a path.

As if a host is sketching the scene in white, the
choicelessness of white, which is why it is so alive.

One two three childs-of-her-skin hang from the
edges, yes, and in them is the color yes.

In her skin there is washing and the taste of white
as in the climax of living now.

About the logic of white, as soon as you *say* white, *whose living experience can only come from space*, she adds passively.

The painter paints white as a form of disappearance sourced from the white that is her.

So that nothing is derived, like the five kinds of eyes or a woman's clothes that can only be cleaned by fire.

The washerwoman looks down. *Down* is a color as she sits with her body because how many of us sit, actually *sit down* in our own body.

Someone leaves. A panel of white looks like a cap
and she is confused.

It could be a bird with a beach plastered on it, the
only spot the deepest bottom of her pupil.

If I throw whiteness on the bird, like a piece of
paper can be a bird.

I touch white out but its geometry blurs, without
guile (in its own nature) between what is so
fervent.

VIII

I wake before dawn and feel the emptiness of blue
in my body.

The country smells blue and little sprouts push
from the earth.

Blue light through hills absorbs into space,
dismantling wind, coloring distant swallows.

Blue may be light but boiled down to the earth of
light so that even its image rides on a tiger.

The quivering of earth vanishes with night.

Blue is a response in its flimsy filmy costume. *Such sweet blue, the* nalo *of blueness,* I mimic.

As if a cloud, like Dombipa, in a practicum of itself, throws the skull of itself to the place of its future self. The ground where it lands becomes frozen in the wake of how much blue is possible.

A lizard-imitating-a-stone, a flower in natural connate sky, as if blue, sprung with the blue of sky, confabulates through beings to the absolute blue of sky.

As if sound were blue and what sound touches also (inevitably) releases the sound of blue's body.

*I live in this ground*, a person says, who keeps the mountain close.

Release is not *into*. His body along with a dimple in the meadow, in plentitude of them and what follows from blue's generosity.

I hear its song in the flakes falling downward but its echo is up and the time of the song even higher up.

The sound of a mountain is soft, like a flock gathering inward. (The continual motion of the flock even down to its belly.)

Each relaxed posture would be all the positive postures that the flock would be able to express.

Sun kneads light into a sound of relating to light, tonsure-snow in sky as it washes over the vastness.

I feel susceptible to snow as if I *am* snow, sun rising over snow, refusing to go to sleep now.

IX

A man has himself crafted in day, as if his
monasticism lay *into* precise day.

He stumbles upon himself, sniff sniff in day, which is
not particularly intelligent, but which is following
his body's refusal.

*I won't be day*, he says. *No!* for him is moving
ahead, as if a man is sculpted to the precise mind of
who he will turn out to be.

As if his man precedes his infant and the sound of
that cry is so very stunning.

The man in the shape of a bird, his perch against sky, is a large space inside me.

Like a bean grows and *there* is sky (the imprimatur of sky) leaving only the action.

If he weren't sky, 'cause the elements are really deities, if he weren't a rim of sky hungering for a space to be.

Seeing beyond the man, flashing back but still beyond the man, seeing a bird whose profile appears to be part of the sky.

When a man is a bird, the left of him shutters and he hides a little.

Then the conviction of *no*, its dead-on precision of place. *No* is accurate, its discipline is accurate, the precision of reverent so solid and solemn.

*No-sky* shatters the *upaya* of mortality, what forms in one's mind, like lace on a tree.

Will the man topple? He hovers on a ledge. A thick sinuous rope hugs the caliber of who he will be there.

X

Devotees mingle among bolts and bolts of fabric as
if in this course they are studying water as all
elements, but not sex. Ears are exclusive of sex.

She lays in a room worrying if her water is enough.
Exclusive looks like branches of a tree.

She becomes the fabric wildly and coils and how
many bolts will fill the bottom of her underworld.

Joy abides in the flooding of the fields, in the bones
of her voice (having metabolized her voice).

The person says no, he doesn't want sex with her, which she feels in her ears, water on people's doorsteps.

Seeing the water hearing, as if *that's* the *that* of the first stage.

A ritual vase holds the cup of your essential water, which is your dead poured slowly but sounding like a roar because you're dead.

As if one's mind, replete with death's form, like when can an animal convene if everything violet embodies a just-broken crucifix.

A consort of energy maps intelligence onto place,
like death is a place and she dances on the place.

The place is dead yet searches in itself for a feeling.

Dancing on a corpse, holding the mace of a baby's
body (what prevails between dead and the clean air
of its body).

Jumpstarting dead, regarding oneself as dead.
Watching myself leap right into her.

XI

A carousel of birds raises a curtain with its beak
and I pop out. (It's a charm on my mother's charm
bracelet.)

Rhinestones on her sweater are flecks of light
shaped like birds whose fingers touch the bottom
of the sea.

An imprint of the bird remains in the sea. *All
animals and beings are the size of the sea,* she is
telling me.

*Lightly, lightly, like froth on sea, we lay our footprints
out over the land.*

As if a bird becomes a bird first inside its own belly.
The ease of its float, so hospitable and safe. Such
nakedness stalks the nothingness of space.

The flight exists and *then* the bird. First, if he is
perched, as if a wrong thing will be completed in
him. (The grip is what's completed, that it has
already happened.)

Like the gait of a bird whose shape scatters. I *see*
the songs instead of hearing them suddenly.

One sings. One sings. Thus he is above himself,
explicating what may slip away.

The logic of a bird is the same as winter sky. Look straight into its eyes and it becomes invisible.

What's this math that makes a double bird but the bird is there anyway pecking at the icicles.

I live in a cave and you can't inherit it. Birds make my cave legible.

Its snow runs wild (which is how the bird can remain quite healthy).

Were it a bird or cloud in the shape of a bird, a
place in sky repelling its illusion in space.

Were I snow falling on birds' wings, am I in its
song, esoteric.

Aloneness is there despite the bird trembling. You
can feel it in its space, what he cannot sing to you.

The bird and I are brothers. Our song is the same.
Throw a spearhead and it's the same. It will *always*
become a flower.

XII

A tendency to real occurrence turns into space. A
person is space. He is white, having been
consumed by fire ravenously.

His eyes lay on his face, like the words of his face
(*what would be taken from me manually in abutment
to my suicide*).

The awareness is itself but also the source. Its
seriality in space follows death along the trail of its
body.

That space between *I* and willing to die, that streak
of *I*, like the nature of the real person habituated to
*I*, but not definite, slightly fishy.

If she thinks about the man or remembers thinking him into experience, a shift occurs, invisible yet definitive, who she is, which is so real.

Because his skin is night now. A skin of wanting peering at a body, a locale.

He separates from time as his swishy body folds, not physically (he is still groping) but the grope looks like a river.

He gropes like a person in the slow motion of a dream, more and more till it is no longer slow, but some preternatural sub-slow, a mirror image of slow's interior.

The man's death appears violent because the man himself is violent, but it is just death.

Being a natural pause between death and its appearance.

I no longer wish for omission, a map of space swallowed by some organic, mechanical process.

The line between impression and breath, awareness and space, digs into space, mixing mind with space.

*Mingling the Threefold Sky*

CONTENTS

WHITE

A man in the dark is a dark man. He calls me from inside the dark water.

That I recognize him in the night without waking is a growing urge of mind.

And then the man appears. I gradually orient toward the man.

The tremulous multiplicity of pause, as if dark is pause, an umbrella of veins puffing and dissolving.

It senses her and stops. She orients towards the stopping like the possibility of a person who *would be* out of darkness.

The stop repeals its form like a word repeals the sensation of something, the *commission* of a sound that holds the language of a word.

Sound fills the cavity and she is there pressing. *I am <u>practicing</u> the word through its darkest cubits of blackness.*

*O sister word! Hold insouciance to any word and you <u>have</u> the word resolved even of the <u>idea</u> of word.*

The man holds the word in the space of himself, in a word made ready for itself.

Such that time is rescued out of her, the long day of time. *I am a thin bone of light, like a duck of light to nothing.*

The *floor* of the word, the long trouble of the word. (She feels from the word a certain mastery of negation.)

*I will live in the word. If its boundary is something produced by the word.*

She tries to feel her floor, but she is thinking about
a cavity, something fluid like a worm and she wants
to *say* the worm.

A moan is a moan and where can it reside if not on
her floor, the speech body of that word.

She jerks it up but trips so that *she* is the floor and
the glue and the shame. *I have a habit of glue,* she
confesses.

A flame of everything sears into shape, which is not
the word, but the colorless basis of its Pure Land.

## YELLOW

A vein of sun hits a woman's cheek. *What is her face,* she wonders, a blush of cheek beneath the long hair of her goldenness.

How sunlight fills the sky is how the mind myelenates appearances to her.

Whose milt is on the edges. It stands in front of sky such that all she sees is sky.

The absolute knowing of sky, weather and sky, like a prerogative that's *said* against which she may stroke her child.

Though she sits facing away, *as if* it is in her, one feels the age of this *away* as her.

The painter paints time locked away from its material, like her own personal face exiled from her face.

As if *away* without location is the real time, the real completion, a recrement of sky, the *other* loneliness of sky.

Rangjung dorge's face. *Its light is not what is in me that way.*

As the moon releases into sky, shedding yellow
back to sky, you see a person's face deep in the
heart of the eye of one.

Day walks out of day losing track of its intelligence,
the part of day held back from day or the end of
his life which is so heartbreaking.

Sound at a distance extends from in front of him.
The arc of his face leaks into shape.

The space between her face, the moon's display of
face. (The features of her belie her apparent face.)

*

The color of day, two figures in a plain, as if two
were possible outside of itself as a number.

As if day were a point dabbed like paint onto the
brief cortex of togetherness.

A pattern of her in yellow, such that she too,
though *he,* the *he* of how they came to be here
forever.

Where clouds are yellow and birds are yellow, a
double portrait of her, which is *them* as who she is.

It's like these two things, the way light throws itself over land, *them* as a pulse, a stream of apposite colors.

The metaphysics of grey within a yellow space, or closeness, the *duo* of her body coming to be the grey.

For this she'd received an empowerment. A doleful space of air. A *prosody* of air.

The belly of the mind leaks the containment of them, as how the painter lifts the *them* of them and simply puts it on a piece of paper.

Waiting is the movement. Waiting is not resting because the aspect of *pair*, a person's hat of hair, the tip of the world at the edge of his hair.

The man is not. He is thinking about something else. His hat facing light holds the tension of his being there.

The skirl of light obscures to fading light. A vague sense of waiting hangs over his elbow.

Now he is home listening to its softness *as if inside me I have finally found my bedfellow.*

*

The fold of a tree over light on a road, if she is *in*
the road, the sense that she would be there
anyway.

An old live tree, like the life of someone screaming,
is the language of the tree pushed outside its form.

What colors grow untouched in her, her and her,
what she sees on the Paris streets.

Old registers hard even in a bit of shade.

What is it in a tree that seems to be erased, as if
emotion were space, and the subtlety that is part
of the tree, the great washing over of space.

The way time holds light on the *inside* of her which
is how color organizes itself toward a person.

It makes me question whether sky is the same
since movement is not limited (I begin to see sky as
limited).

Fifty three skies settle in my backyard may simply
be sky pouring out sky.

The painter's mind meets tree and recognizes where there *should* be a tree but it seems like a real tree.

Tree is how time rests back on its own mind.

Because trees need repeatability. Its eye is that prostration. *I will catch my eye in the rigpa of her eye.*

Sacraments repeat in the full verse of eyes, the laying on of an eye, a closed eye or even an eye asleep.

## RED

Someone paints a dream thinking it is the person,
cuts out the dream and the dream becomes its
word.

*Now the person will know and his word will have the
letters of an eastern province.*

He is tied to this loosely as if beyond the chance of
knowing, a bodice of time (angling loosely) down
the crevice of his back, loosely.

A man in a horn makes a home for himself in the
horn such that the space in the horn opens to the
vast expanse of his own mudra.

Looking east into space as it pales into sky, he is hearing her painting her but not from the source of her hearing him hear her.

A rattle, disassembled by his mind, appears at the flounce of her skirt-line.

*Can't* also. Can't relates to time as an index. *Can I fit? If I were who I am?* The equation nags a memory.

What is the equation for the mind outside the time, the Sugata of time, each *tissue* of time.

The sound and the struggle to receive it in his body, like its bloodtype is wrong for a person with his body.

It's a situation of her blood becoming ready to be her blood, *after* the pogrom, *after* the sea. Actually red is Word.

*Shtetl* is the adjective. *Can't* is not east, nor made from the red of tongues.

What translates from the sea (because her ankles hold the sea) now *able* to be a sea, steadying up the sea.

The fib of the girl groping through herself, because real hearing is just itself, cheap like the wrong mother.

*I am swimming for ten minutes,* cries the Ocean God's one-eyed children.

Though the habit of time makes red seem almost hollow, the dakinis say, *no, please, our joy is red. Outside blessing there is no red.*

I tear up. I realize who she is in the sconce of her red body, like an offering to sky or how the dark sea holds up sky.

The intimacy of red is like hearing the sound of
your birth.

Or the birth of red, like at Yale where red is a
park.

What pertains outside of what we think of as a
color (if red were a smell and we put it in a jar, and
someone opens the jar).

If sound is red, coming to synthesis in a word, the
word lifts off its word, the clarity of mind raised to
the red of the word.

Her body is red and her penis, also, is a thick red.

Like you could vacuum red into your hand let's say.

Fucking red, sliding her hand up the thick course of all procreations of red fathers.

HOW-at-large is how the mother dissolves. She *clothes* the bars that tie her land to red.

Breaking back the skin of its tip, some say it's the cut itself, the brave cut of red in the hollow of its mind.

The mind of red cusses red, backwards toward the front of its tongue.

*The lungs of the sea are hollow of devotion.* One keeps its body close like a vajra "dick" of red's secret body.

Tongue, mouth, body are as if painted red, but gushingly so
that the green of red, the deep soft of green's pure body
becomes red's Luscious Body.

## GREEN

I look out on a hill. It is bald with exuberance of old decaying objects.

A shallow hill and sense of day dissolving is a lateral memory of time.

A shrub is alive, its decay is alive. The slope of the hill may not be selected into finitudes.

In a cycle of empty light, no birds land.

I see a house of rolling hills as if the hills had taken
refuge but had not taken a vow of refuge.

Hills and hills of bedding in light, the *taking* of light,
the laying down of light.

The observance of the vow is definitely green,
though below the ground dark movement churns,
as if the spirits of light are upset.

A pretense of green, which is unfortunate, like the
mistress of the beds whose greens purvey a chakra
that can't settle.

*The engine of green is continuous,* she says. (You are sitting in a room watching a broadcast on a small screen near the ceiling.)

Many people are there, like a corporation of *there* (the sense of *there* is inside them, which they now realize).

Their ribcages have come ajar, but instantaneously and with conviction, like *This ajar is final.*

As a woman teems into the room, what stands as her own body. Mind implodes its fulfillment body.

*

Windows play to light and glass and hair and
pointing, but the heel of the point is old and its
green is old.

Sucking green, like at night when she sucks the hell
out of her body.

Her form stands inside the essence of her body, a
symbol of space like a letter that stands for space.

The dawning of an arm through a glass of green, a
species of pirouette on the point of her final green.

She feels stuck in the glass, both sensing its meaning, but like a dream, sensing a peripheral lurking falseness.

*In the wild of glass, how can I be born in so much glass?* (The rectitude of her sash has long been known by the girl.)

*Anything formed loses nascence,* someone cries. Crystal becomes a deity, rice a snake lashing about as a protector.

Movement has stopped but the agony of time, a dancer stands in the glass of her toe shoe's time, like an *asana* of time.

The still of a dancer's back, if it is *of movement,* is
not an image of my feeling.

Because there needs to be green. *That's the
mandala inside my whole body.*

*The nuance of the color will convene in me. Its word is
laid in me.* Quiet morning light brings a bowl of it
to her forehead.

Day is her support, the first position of mind, a
turn-out of mind so that day may grow long.

## BLUE

A paradigm of phrase, such as a woman bending, whether it be evening or fall, in the slow motion of bending toward something.

The awareness is in her neck and gentle *down* of softness as if the profile of her face faces a separate direction from her face.

As if her face stands beside its own absolute loveliness, revealed in *down* whose axis is not the axis of the intelligence of her body.

Her body sits down in the weight of a person's shell whose full curving masses become, some say, the *racial quality* of the shell.

Race is blue as in the catching of a mind, a shallow remainder of mind deep in its inheritance.

Whose *dristi* settles, both *in* herself, if her mind spreads to his through her body.

That a *dristi* can be queen combines a long history of sewing, how her character can stop (though the motion of bending does not stop).

As a painter paints the lack of occurrence of mind, she goes in which is instantly the real mind.

*Am* is the assessment. *(I am new, clean as sky.)*

Because boredom is open and joy is open, like if I am a bird and then tomorrow the intervening presence of myself.

Whose scent is in the *tukdam*. The bird grows small but she is dead.

The awareness is there and the vicinity, too, holds the bird.

*She's a shot bird. (Shot is a value.)*

*I am in the purview of tenderness,* she's crying.

*I am a broken bird. I am raped and then I am a bird again.*

Is heard through a clearing, but it is just the bird and she shines its light so prettily like the repeated sequence of a waterfall.

＊

Here is night and death lies bleeding, the deepest
black of light at the edge of a sparrow's forehead.

Its dark internal quest pushes toward what is exact
 in him, to say a state of dark at the bottom of his
pillow.

And there's something else that I can't remember,
a holocaust of birds being the blackness of pale
color.

The space of black is the barren essence of a color,
like pain or *his* mind that we can no longer say is a
color.

Blackness is alive, palpable in an accused person. A guard senses it trembling.

The black of an iris makes black out of light. *It's the kingdom of black blowing black across the fields.*

What is this word, like a domino of air, which they cannot know, cannot take. Light enters through its scales.

*We welcome you into air,* they say, but they have no idea of air, they are just *saying* air.

The guard sees a scale and says _this is the scale._ Its stillness is black and its water is black.

_Like a bodice of death is effluvial and lightly striated colors._

_Said_ and its air that comes to him from somewhere. Saraha is the name of one, whose arrows have the thickness of one.

_Is pierced in my hair (or half of hair)_ excoriates the poverty of its word.

He sees the mind in the word as a sudden
realization, not just the vision but as a particular
situation.

Like time exists in time, but due to the power of
infinity of ordinary errors stays fully dissolved in
confusion.

*Past doesn't exist,* the guard repeats. (The struggle
to extort a sense of how *exist* can be.)

The blue motion of a star, the torture of the star.
In the ash of it is a word, but not conceived, as in
the slow fingernails of his father.

*

Blue land falls to dusk before dusk falls, like a taste that opens in your heart.

A wind of blue settles with sky as it fades over the land.

A gum-tree is quiet. Air absorbs its light.

As if a penny were dead, slow in slow night. The slow vase and touch of winter.

His view of mud in the full jelly of the land, blue or
black as he calls to her primitively.

Shadows of time pour out their place so as to not
encounter anything.

Shapes at a distance may be sky making arcs, a
vagina aroused to sky and open to sky's subtleties.

Blue is space. Dusk is source. In a lapse of wind,
the *skin* of rain hovering, a word that has departed.

Lust in the wet land. (I fish into my mind.)

Mud in particular stands beside each light particle differently.

Night is light. Night is so light. If you touch it it turns into memory.

He stares into blue as it softens into *not blue,* making distance from elaborations of blue-on-blue, blue-on-*not-blue.*

Dusk in a hill dissolves into a cow, visible but indistinguishable, like consciousness.

The cow has an umbrella. *The dakinis are playing their drums,* people say.

A rainbow is the deities welcoming the cow back. The local wisdom deities are so happy to see the cow.

The cow allows its happiness to be seen.

LATE WORK 2014-2018

# *Introduction*

Late work (the poetry I began writing in 2014) addresses a different part of the brain than my earlier work.

The element of space directs itself no longer to wisdom mind but to lesser-exalted areas of the self.

That human beings are primarily relational takes on new significance.

Formerly silence was *in* the word and *was* the word (introverted). Now it is also referential (extroverted).

> New Year's Eve
> listen—
> snow is falling[1]

Sensation becomes memory.

---

[1] *Pale Sky*, p. 10, (page references to the original publication; see bibliography for details).

What erupts may be from the reptilian brain but may also stem from more highly evolved areas.

Meaning extends beyond the word into clusters of words, sentences and remainders after the sentences have passed.

> The mind of the woman is warm, her sweaters and chickens and all the places on the boat . . .

> "Hello," Unn offers.

> "What?" shouts the woman.[2]

Meaning finally is useful. Before, it not only was not useful, it obstructed what was useful.

Before there was the boat. Now there's the other shore.

The *device*—thinking you know what it means— becomes authenticated by the text—you *do* know what it means.

> She wondered if the fact that things ceased to exist in her meant that they ceased to exist.

> Does time cease to exist or does it flow

---

[2]*Sunny Day, Spring*, p. 3.

parallel to what looks like one's existence?

What is one's existence? What is the relation
between time and one's existence?[3]

It means what it means to you, but meaning is
*intended* whereas in the earlier work, the flow *toward*
meaning was simply bait.

---

[3]*Ezekiel*, p. 78.

from
## *Sunny Day, Spring*

Unn had been reading. Light from the dawning
sky fell upon her book. "The days are such that I
hardly need a lamp," she was thinking when she
heard a click. "That would be Töl."

Unn returned to her book and to the deep
silence of the day.

"*Was* that Töl?" Aware suddenly of how quiet the
house seemed, she paused. "Was that today? Maybe
it was yesterday."

Unn tried to remember precisely when she'd
heard the lock on the door click, but she couldn't be
sure.

She closed her eyes. Recently she'd read—the
article was in the *New York Times*—a war victim
who'd been tortured was being treated for post
traumatic stress. Though he'd suffered physical pain,
his main symptom—what was intolerable to him and
wouldn't leave him—was the loss of a sense of time.
He simply had no idea of where he was in space, of
how much time had passed or how long any activity

would take. When the therapist slowly said, "Take your time, Sergio, we have plenty of time," it was as if his sobbing would never stop.

from
*Ezekiel*

"My eyes are watering it's so cold."

Her cheeks were flushed. He thought he saw them flicker for a second.

"It's just my eyes. Everything else is fine," she added, blinking rapidly as if the action itself would warm them.

"We're lucky it's so clear."

Luciano didn't feel like talking. He was looking at the sky *and* looking at Ezekiel.

Silence filled the air as though the universe were voiceless now.

As though a core, a point of reference, had irrevocably been torn away.

When it fanned out spreading higher and higher and higher, it left Luciano and Ezekiel in darkness.

from
## *Pale Sky*

*From the first moment I enter the* zendo
*I am changed.*

*The fragrance, the clarity stir a deadness in me that
I've lugged around and lugged around.*

*I recognize it with my teeth, behind my ears, between
my toes, the bottoms of my feet.*

*It is startling and immediate.*

*The same sense—almost a nostalgia—filters through
the air, the grounds, the trees.*

*People talking, jays cawing. It's just a caw but its
rawness makes a point and repeats the point and
repeats the point.*

*I'm hearing the empty beginning, before the person or
the jay get involved.*

*Even the air rattles with its mind.*

*The sound is fresh. It stays cool in the heat. Beyond
immaculate, its cleanness is original.*

*The wind in the trees is crisper. Leaves are more
defined.*

*Colors are subtler as if elsewhere, even elsewhere in
the same range of mountains, this feeling is quelled by
the lack of an inherited intelligence.*

*The legacy of mind, big mind, Zen mind, establishes
the legitimacy, even of the pansies.*

Traipsing in my getas down the rain-drenched path, my muscles know precisely the beyond-knowing of its importance.

Like a nocturnal bird seeks a safe place to rest during the day in a vacant attic.

Chirps and caws sprinkle through the air as dawn hits the trees and pale sky colors the brick wall that I am staring at.

It's this path but it's the sky and the eon's sky and the yuga's sky and all the yugas' skies.

*"O n e . . ." she said mentally,* listening to the soft stream of air through her nostrils.

"T w o . . ." started at the top while the air was in her nose but the sound, slower now and more nasal, seemed to be coming from her throat.

"T h r e e . . ." though the "three" came as an afterthought.

The person to her right was leaning forward on his knees trying to fit a third *zafu* under his buttocks, but the second one kept slipping out making the third one lopsided.

Eliza stayed still. Steadying her gaze she continued counting exhales, but her mind went to the day— she'd so wanted to make a personal connection.

"Is there anything I should bring?" She twiddled a strand of hair too tightly around a finger.

He yawned with his jaw, without opening his mouth. "You'll be doing the personal lists." It wasn't really an answer.

Then he'd simply stood absorbed in looking out.

She wished he wouldn't shift around on his pillows so much.

*"This morning early Roshi, peacefully, died. We continue our efforts along with all beings."*

The words entered the hall toward the beginning of second period.

Silence. More silence. Bristling silence.

But it was soft.

New Year's Eve
listen—
snow is falling

*We just sit. It is like something happening in the great sky.*

*To express our way along with all beings—we sit for this and it will always be the same.*

*Whatever kind of bird, the sky doesn't care. That is the mind transmitted from the Buddha to us.*

Avalokiteshvara Bodhisattva, *practicing deeply* Prajña Paramita . . .

from
*Elm*

A nighthawk's cry startled her.

As if in response Machie moaned.

Her hair, loose now, lay over one cheek and the palm of her hand over that.

It was her right hand. The long middle finger reached her jaw.

Her other hand fell toward the corner of the bed.

It was a child's hand.

"Take me to bed." Machie had said it first.

The warmth of her, undeveloped, a little skittish, had been unlike the smooth, clean-burning warmth of the woman she was now.

Her dark places were warm.

Sometimes even now . . .

She could be sixteen any minute.

"Can I know you? Will you live?"

Once she'd seen a picture of very young Machie in roller skates laughing, arm slung around a boy.

But her eyes had looked old. Her laughter somehow stilted.

Living old, a child lives out her oldness so that when she comes of age she has the knowledge to be young originally.

A scar on Machie's shoulder took the shape of violets.

Despite the scar the shoulder was young and fresh.

Might it be that the scar, the result of her experience, richened the flavor of Machie's innocence?

The scent of a baby came to her. It had the close warm softness of sleep.

A faint wild crying from the violets ebbed and rose, ebbed and rose.

The piquant odor of blood, Machie's menstrual blood, rose from the depths of her slumber.

The scent was full with the presence of Machie's womanliness.

"It's like blood that wants a baby," Naoko'd once observed, meaning only that it was a rich, good blood.

"Don't say that," Machie'd smarted.

Along with the smell, pungent yet sweet, was the memory of the smell mixed as it was with their past.

"How did you lose your virginity," Machie'd teased, egging Naoko on with question after question.

She looked so new. The undone braid fanned over her mouth.

It wore an echo that carried time like the condensed feelings of sadness that made the air crack.

"How many women have you kissed?"

Machie had asked and she had asked but they were just sounds to cover the amazement of their passion.

Outside there'd been thrushes singing themselves crazy.

"Let's find a less-musical bird," Machie had joked, rolling out of bed, pulling on her jeans.

"Okay, let's." But the neighborhood was transfixed.

"So how many women have you kissed?" insisted Machie in dazed sobriety.

Lying face up with her legs spread wide, bedding pushed down, Machie slept on.

Her head had slid to the far left edge.

Lips pursed, the usually broad mouth seemed almost to form a heart, puckered at the center and totally unlike her.

Her bones were resting. Even her teeth seemed to be resting.

from
*Mary's Eyes*

i

cold and snow. the sound of snow falling. the young
novice's eyes
it's (the) forgiveness that she notices
(an old noticing) she feels


thinks about Christ. will she marry him. she has already
married him (she feels)
asks if she is sure


[bells sound in the background]

figures appear. the clink of plates, spoons,
hush of nuns eating
the *rule* of the meal (omitting) the meal
the weight of the prioress's eyes


readings turn to time (the word *Mary* repeated)
verse empty of her suddenly

ii

a tall girl and her girl (their "astrology" of brotherhood)
the eyes of one watching from a second-floor window
what the watching girl is thinking versus the couple—
walking, carrying books, talking
loneliness and time. more loneliness and time


"crippled time" she muses opening the sash for a better
view
as if time and her ribs—as if time *stopped* her ribs
"see" she presses placing a hand on one

INTERLUDE

alone in an open room
water and wind (their) hardness in time
wearing out time replaced she feels with time
the freshness of wet blows around her lightly

[her sense of the sea (awareness) of time (her presence in
the room) co-adjacent with time]


her dog too on the rug below
one eye opening then closing (seemingly) content
the sand covering its body and what the sand *says* about
its life
the dog's ear and what the dog is noticing (waiting) for
something to end


sees the waves of the sea melt into sea
its song vanishing to nothing
the rhythm of the vanishing repetitive (prayerful)
the earth (too) which the sea hears

listens to sea (the sound of the sea breathing) the
implacability of *sea* time
its power and its blueness circling her like a tiger
the tiger's immaculate stealth

iv

blue late-April sky, sound of waves lashing
the girl's jaw remembering something ungraspable
the sea itself ungraspable


thin (soft) time which she dreads
the *coming* of harm, ripening and then, moonlit
*coming* to know (*coming* being its own naked color)


"soon" she thinks but it's vague
the upshot of vague like a portion of a color


notices sky, a shadow of a tree, the mind of the tree
transferred to a form
what the form may imply and whether or not she
generalizes its significance
*reads* the clothes for clues

sees Jesus in his robes rising a little (bowing) toward
her (slightly)
sees herself seeing the vivid reality of his form
the body of Christ (touching) it with sight
(its) aperture and tone with regard to so much happening


the event—Jesus rising—and then again rising—
"toward her" *had been there* the first time (she is realizing)
as if his life took place
(in her mind a lion yawns)


[but it's clapping. someone is bowing to an act seemingly
ended
the impossibility of blue (since it stands for itself) ending]


authority of blue (standing for itself) attentive (to) what
we *call* color
which may have taken place previous to time or even
in some other time
"what is my color before there was color"
ransacks blue as if it were light instead

## *Introduction*

These poems are written as *tanka* (Japanese: "short song"). In terms of treatment of subject, *tanka* resemble the sonnet. Like a sonnet they employ a turn which marks the transition from the examination of an image to the examination of a personal response. Instead of a *haiku*-like flash of insight, *tanka* quietly recognize things as they are.

from
*City of Sleep*

It's quiet outside
during the night it rained
but it's quiet
I'm alone
no one knows my thoughts.

Black clouds through gray pre-dawn sky
move forebodingly toward the hills
sounds of night linger
I want to stay awhile, listen
what prevents me I wonder?

Old now, I live in the city:

A temple bell wakes me
*it's not your bell—you don't have to move*
I tell myself as I'm turning over
it's dawn, the sky is pink
thank God.

I hear you cough from the other room
while you are having breakfast
and I think how it could be that
you are no longer in the other room—
what will I listen to then?

*It will die soon anyway*
I think, snapping it off
before anyone sees—thus,
because of my rashness . . .
o the damage done by my rashness.

Inside me
is a ghost of me
I saw it yesterday—
cold, unwell
it had blue eyes.

You and I, sweet bird
hang together in this spot
you stare out
I stare out
please don't forget to return.

# Responding to a *tanka* by Saigyō (1118-1190)

Ten Poems for the Lady-in-Waiting of the Second Rank
*Adding one more*
*to the graves*
*at the foot of Boat Hill,*
*we make you*
*"someone of the past"*

Your "someone of the past"
speaks with such sorrow, Saigyō
as for me it won't be long . . . pray for me in
my life to come!

# Chronologies

*A Personal Chronology of External Life Circumstances*

1942: Born in St. Louis, Missouri's Jewish Hospital.

1947-53: Elementary school in University City, a suburb of St. Louis.

1954-57: Hanley Junior High School in University City.

1958-60: University City Senior High School (avid reader, diary writer and aspiring pianist studying with Harold Zabrach).

1960-61: University of Florida, Gainesville (study piano, music history, composition, theory).

1961-62: Hebrew University, Jerusalem (study Hebrew, Torah and piano at the Jerusalem Academy of Music).

1962-64: BA in English at Northwestern University. Receive Ford Foundation Fellowship to study linguistics at the University of Texas at Austin.

1964: Choose instead to study Middle English at the University of California, Berkeley; meet Arthur Weiner, fellow graduate student in English and reader for the poet Thom Gunn.

1965: Arthur and I marry.

1966: Receive a secondary teaching credential from U.C. Berkeley.

1966-68: Enjoy teaching high school English at Ygnacio Valley High and Pleasant Hill High; win "Teacher of the Year" Award from three education faculties (Stanford, Berkeley, San Francisco State). Have a harpsichord built and begin studying harpsichord with a very gifted teacher, Jean Nandi, a student of Gustav Leonhardt.

November 1968: Arthur and I separate; I begin sitting zazen at the Berkeley Zendo (part of the San Francisco Zen Center).

Summer 1969: Attend Summer Practice Period at Tassajara Zen Mountain Center with Suzuki-roshi.

Fall 1969: Move into the Berkeley Zendo; and, encouraged by Jean Nandi, begin a second BA, in music, at UC Berkeley.

1971: Move to San Francisco Zen Center and Tassajara Zen Mountain Center in order to practice Zen full-time; ordained a lay disciple of Suzuki-roshi.

1980: Leave Zen Center after eleven years, realizing that my practice needs to be *writing*.[1] I had already abandoned the formal practice of music, consciously dedicating my musical ability to writing, selling my harpsichord and donating the proceeds to purchase a great temple bell, crafted in Japan, for Zen Center.

1980: I move to an apartment on Haight Street and begin writing daily, publishing poems in small literary journals. Become friends with Beau Beausoleil, Leslie Scalapino and Merry Benezra.

---

[1] *Moon of the Swaying Buds* describes how I came to this decision. Through Zen I discover "Yes Practice": only doing those things I can say Yes to with my whole body and mind. By then, however, "I am through with Zen Center. I need to define my own regime. Zen Center has had it with me anyway. I am told privately that unless my attitude changes, I will not be accepted for Fall Practice Period. Indeed, my attitude has changed but not in the direction that would pique my interest in Fall Practice Period" (*Moon of the Swaying Buds*, 2017, p.392).

1980: At my first poetry reading at Beau Beauso-leil's San Francisco bookstore, Robert Duncan is in attendance and asks, "Would you read that again?" He encourages me to send what I had just read to a new poetry journal, *Credences,* published by the Poetry Collection at the University at Buffalo. My work appears in the inaugural issue along with poetry by Duncan himself.

1982-1986: Leslie Scalapino arranges for me to move into the apartment next to hers in Berkeley and we give joint poetry readings and visit other poets, including a memorable trip to Albuquerque in 1986 for a reading at the Living Batch Bookstore and to visit one of my favorite poets, Mei-Mei Berssenbrugge. I work as a personal assistant for Billy and Alice Shap-iro and begin publishing books of poetry with small, independent presses.

1982-1993: Yoga-based meditation practice with Self Realization Fellowship. I am attracted to this heart-based practice, which complements the mind-based Zen I knew; I especially appreciate that this community, founded by Paramahansa Yogananda in the 1920s, is led by women.

1985-1990 Complete MA in Clinical Psychology
at John F. Kennedy University; meet Brendan
Collins, former Benedictine monk, photographer,
teacher and psychologist.

1990: Brendan and I marry; I begin private
practice as psychotherapist; continue publishing with
small presses.

1995: Meet Adzom Paylo Rinpoche, meditation
master in the Nyingma tradition of Tibetan
Buddhism, and begin a concentrated study of
Tibetan Buddhism; complete the *Longchen Nyingthig
Ngondro* under his direction and guidance. This form
of Buddhism brings together the heart *and* mind
practice I have long sought.

1997-continuing: After the closing of so many
small independent presses, Brendan and I establish
Night Crane Press; I continue writing early every
morning, working as a psychotherapist, practicing
Tibetan Buddhism, and enjoying living with Brendan.

*An Internal History of My Relationship with Language*

"The literary persona who enacts the poet's struggle can be glimpsed, always, in one early work that Ted Hughes calls the 'first,' which contains, in a single image, 'a package of precisely folded, multiple meanings.' The origin of this image is a trauma, usually hidden from the writer's consciousness, that partakes in a wholly personal way of some destructive aspect of cultural life."[1]

The dates are vague. We live on an army base in North Carolina where my father, Charles Sher, is stationed.

While he is overseas, I live with my mother, her three volatile sisters, her absent father, nervous-breakdown-prone mother, and a slightly older, noisy and aggressive male cousin. In this household—I am two—I begin stuttering and am diagnosed with

---

[1]Diane Middlebrook, *Her Husband: Ted Hughes and Sylvia Plath—A Marriage* (New York: Penguin, 2003), p. 245.

a "nervous breakdown." The symptoms—stuttering, hypervigilance and nonadaptability to change—are consistent with recent research on pre-school children in traumatic, disruptive, unpredictable environments.

I am removed to the apartment of my paternal grandmother who says to my mother, "You can live here but I'm not paying for her milk."

With his impressive purple heart my war veteran father returns. "Honey, that's your father." "No it's not. *This* is my father," I say, pointing to his photograph. I believe I am four.

A primary memory is sitting on an outside step striving toward collecting all my words and feeling extremely frustrated that I do not know how to write.

My hysterical mother and war-traumatized father fight constantly (about money and sexual transgressions on both parts).

I act out in elementary school. Feel very very ugly. Take refuge in reading the interesting books provided by my mother.

I rock in bed, at my desk in school, in my rocking chair when I am reading.

Begin to adjust socially in 9th grade, become a cheerleader and am liked by boys, but I cannot think analytically and only do average in my classes, which feels not only humiliating but somehow wrong (incorrect).

In 10th grade an English teacher compliments what she calls a "parallel structure" that I use inadvertently. On the spot I decide to become a writer but am discouraged by my father who says, "Oh everyone wants to be *that*."

Thinking and writing analytically continue to be problems all the way through graduate school, though at Northwestern I devised a way to pass written exams, receive my B.A. and a Ford Foundation Fellowship to study linguistics.

Meanwhile in high school, in an outside study, I test at the 99th percentile in math and language, and have been in a longitudinal study for gifted children ever since. (I am now 77.)

Oddly (to me) I feel I "belong" in the gifted group yet consistently my drifting mind and grades do not back that up.

Eventually I have the following thought: "I CAN'T see white like everyone else, but the black I see is not nothing. It is rich and full of music." I begin to feature it in my stabs at writing (having still the sense that I do not know what I'm doing, but liking the result).

The thought that it is something is a turning point.

Based on recent research on the neurological effect of trauma, my frontal lobes probably were dysfunctional, but my implicit memories and awareness were not dysfunctional. Since this is all I have, I lavish my attention on THAT.

I discover that I am hyper-aware of aspects about language that most people ignore.

With years of disciplined Buddhist practice behind me, I force myself to write from the *right* side of my brain and discover a whole new relationship with words.

In retrospect I feel that were it not for the trauma—
whose effect was at the forefront through my thirties,
into my forties and to some extent is *still* present—I
would not have seen, certainly not so clearly, the
contents of the space brightened by a shut-down left
frontal cortex.

I feel grateful for the passion that insisted on a way,
and eventually found a way, and made it *my* WAY.

# Bibliography

*Poetry Books by Gail Sher organized by phase*

1. RADICAL LANGUAGE EXPERIMENTS, 1982-1997

*From another point of view the woman seems to be resting.* San Francisco: Trike, 1982.

*(As) on things which (headpiece) touches the Moslem.* San Francisco: Square Zero, 1982.

*Rouge to beak having me.* Paris: Moving Letters Press, 1983.

*Broke Aide.* Providence: Burning Deck, 1985.

*Cops.* Berkeley: Little Dinosaur, 1988.

*KUKLOS.* Providence: Paradigm Press, 1995.

*la.* Boulder: Rodent Press, 1996.

*Marginalia.* Chicago: Rodent Press, 1997.

*Early Work.* Emeryville, CA: Night Crane Press, 2016.

2   ASIAN-INFLUENCED WORK, 2001-2017

*Moon of the Swaying Buds.* Emeryville, CA:
Night Crane Press, 2001. Third Edition, 2017.

*Look at That Dog All Dressed Out in Plum Blossoms.*
Emeryville, CA: Night Crane Press, 2002.

*RAGA.* Emeryville, CA: Night Crane Press, 2004.

*redwing daylong daylong.* Emeryville, CA: Night Crane
Press, 2004.

*Once There Was Grass.* Emeryville, CA: Night Crane
Press, 2004.

*DOHĀ.* Emeryville, CA: Night Crane Press, 2005.

*Watching Slow Flowers.* Emeryville, CA: Night Crane
Press, 2006.

*The Haiku Masters: Four Poetic Diaries.* Emeryville, CA:
Night Crane Press, 2008.

*Five Haiku Narratives* Emeryville, CA: Night Crane
Press. 2015.[1]

---

[1] Contains the following out-of-print chapbooks written between
1996-2002: *Like a Crane at Night* (1996); *One Bug ... One Mouth ... Snap!*
(1997); *Saffron Wings* (1998); *Fifty Jigsawed Bones* (1999); *Lines: The Life of
a Laysan Albatross* (2002).

3  THE WISDOM-MIND COLLECTION, 2008-2013

*though actually it is the same earth.* Emeryville, CA: Night Crane Press, 2008.

*The Tethering of Mind to Its Five Permanent Qualities.* Emeryville, CA: Night Crane Press, 2009.

*Mother's Warm Breath.* Emeryville, CA: Night Crane Press, 2010.

*White Bird.* Emeryville, CA: Night Crane Press, 2010.

*The Bardo Books.* Emeryville, CA: Night Crane Press, 2011.

*Figures in Blue.* Emeryville, CA: Night Crane Press, 2012.

*The Twelve Nidānas.* Emeryville, CA: Night Crane Press, 2012.

*Mingling the Threefold Sky.* Emeryville, CA: Night Crane Press, 2013.

## 4 LATE WORK, 2014-PRESENT

*Sunny Day, Spring.* Emeryville, CA: Night Crane Press, 2014.

*Ezekiel.* Emeryville, CA: Night Crane Press, 2015.

*Pale Sky.* Emeryville, CA: Night Crane Press, 2015.

*Elm.* Emeryville, CA: Night Crane Press, 2016.

*Mary's Eyes.* Emeryville, CA: Night Crane Press, 2018.

*City of Sleep* (in press)

*Publications by Gail Sher by date, 1980-2020*

PROSE BOOKS

*Reading Gail Sher.* Emeryville, CA: Night Crane Press, 2016.

*Poetry, Zen and the Linguistic Unconscious.* Emeryville, CA: Night Crane Press, 2016.

*Writing the Fire: Yoga and the Art of Making Your Words Come Alive.* New York: Random House/Bell Tower, 2006.

*The Intuitive Writer: Listening to Your Own Voice.* New York: Penguin, 2002.

*One Continuous Mistake: Four Noble Truths for Writers.* New York: Penguin, 1999.

*From a Baker's Kitchen: Techniques and Recipes for Quality Baking in the Home Kitchen.* Twentieth Anniversary Edition. New York: Marlow & Co., 2004.

*From a Baker's Kitchen: Techniques and Recipes for Professional Quality Baking in the Home Kitchen.* Berkeley: Aris Books, 1984.

POETRY BOOKS

*City of Sleep* (in press).

*Gail Sher Poetry & Poetics 1980-2020.* Emeryville, CA:
Night Crane Press, 2020

*Mary's Eyes.* Emeryville, CA: Night Crane Press, 2018.

*Elm.* Emeryville, CA: Night Crane Press, 2016.

*Early Work.* Emeryville, CA: Night Crane Press, 2016.

*Ezekiel.* Emeryville, CA: Night Crane Press, 2015.

*Pale Sky.* Emeryville, CA: Night Crane Press, 2015.

*Five Haiku Narratives.* Emeryville, CA: Night Crane
Press. 2015.

*Sunny Day, Spring.* Emeryville, CA: Night Crane Press,
2014.

*Mingling the Threefold Sky.* Emeryville, CA: Night
Crane Press, 2013.

*The Twelve Nidānas.* Emeryville, CA: Night Crane
Press, 2012.

*Figures in Blue.* Emeryville, CA: Night Crane Press, 2012.

*The Bardo Books.* Emeryville, CA: Night Crane Press, 2011.

*White Bird.* Emeryville, CA: Night Crane Press, 2010.

*Mother's Warm Breath.* Emeryville, CA: Night Crane Press, 2010.

*The Tethering of Mind to Its Five Permanent Qualities.* Emeryville, CA: Night Crane Press, 2009.

*though actually it is the same earth.* Emeryville, CA: Night Crane Press, 2008.

*The Haiku Masters: Four Poetic Diaries.* Emeryville, CA: Night Crane Press, 2008.

*Who, a* Licchavi. Emeryville, CA: Night Crane Press, 2007.

*Calliope.* Emeryville, CA: Night Crane Press, 2007.

*old* dri's *lament.* Emeryville, CA: Night Crane Press, 2007.

*The Copper Pheasant Ceases Its Call.* Emeryville, CA: Night Crane Press, 2007.

*East Wind Melts the Ice.* Emeryville, CA: Night Crane Press, 2007.

*Watching Slow Flowers*. Emeryville, CA: Night Crane Press, 2006.

*DOHĀ*. Emeryville, CA: Night Crane Press, 2005.

*RAGA*. Emeryville, CA: Night Crane Press, 2004.

*Once There Was Grass*. Emeryville, CA: Night Crane Press, 2004.

*redwing daylong daylong*. Emeryville, CA: Night Crane Press, 2004.

*Birds of Celtic Twilight: A Novel in Verse*. Emeryville, CA: Night Crane Press, 2004.

*Look at That Dog All Dressed Out in Plum Blossoms*. Emeryville, CA: Night Crane Press, 2002.

*Lines: The Life of a Laysan Albatross*. Emeryville, CA: Night Crane Press, 2002 [reprinted in *Five Haiku Narratives*].

*Moon of the Swaying Buds* (Limited First Edition). Emeryville, CA: Night Crane Press, 2001.

*Moon of the Swaying Buds*. San Francisco: Edgework, 2002.

*Moon of the Swaying Buds.* Third Edition. Emeryville, CA: Night Crane Press, 2017.

*Fifty Jigsawed Bones: A Sea Turtle's Life.* Emeryville, CA: Night Crane Press, 2001 [reprinted in *Five Haiku Narratives*].

*Saffron Wings.* Berkeley: Night Crane Press, 1998 [reprinted in *Five Haiku Narratives*]. .

*One bug . . . one mouth . . . snap! A Year in the Life of a Turtle.* Berkeley: Night Crane Press, 1997 [reprinted in *Five Haiku Narrative*].

*Marginalia.* Chicago: Rodent Press, 1997.

*la.* Boulder: Rodent Press, 1996.

*Like a Crane at Night.* Berkeley: Night Crane Press, 1996 [reprinted in *Five Haiku Narratives*].

*KUKLOS.* Providence: Paradigm Press, 1995.

*Cops.* Berkeley: Little Dinosaur, 1988.

*Broke Aide.* Providence: Burning Deck, 1985.

*Rouge to beak having me.* Paris: Moving Letters Press, 1983.

*(As) on things which (headpiece) touches the Moslem.*
San Francisco: Square Zero, 1982.

*From another point of view the woman seems to be
resting.* San Francisco: Trike, 1982.

PERIODICALS & ANTHOLOGIES

"Excerpt from *Blue*." *Al-Mutanabbi Street Starts Here.*
Eds. Beau Beausoleil & Deema K. Shehabi. Oakland,
CA: PM Press, 2012. 71. Print.

"Hundred-Stanza Renga" [with Andrew Schelling],
*Simply Haiku,* 8.2, Autumn 2010.

"can't touch you" [with David Rice]. *The Tanka
Journal* 14. Tokyo: Nihon Kajin Club [Japan Tanka
Poets' Club], 1999. 10. Print.

"Lovers" [nine poems]. *Generator* 8.1: *A Magazine
of International Experimental Visual and Language
Material.* Cleveland, OH: Generator Press, 1998. n.p.
Print.

"Autumn" [includes Japanese translation]. *Ashiya
International Haiku Festa 1998.* [Award]. Ashiya,
Hyogo, Japan: 1998. 36. Print.

"Against the longed-for clouds" [with David Rice].
*Tanka Splendor 1997.* [Award]. Gualala, CA: AHA
Books, 1997. n.p. Print.

"Fallout." [Honorable Mention]. *Hiroshima Haiku and
Tanka Competition,* 1997. n.p. Print.

"Silent snow." *One Breath: Haiku Society of America 1995 Members' Anthology.* New York: Haiku Society of America, 1996. 14. Print,

"Basho." *Black Bough* 8. Flemington, NJ: 1996. 5. Print.

"The Paintings of Social Concern." *Juxta* 4. Charlottesville, VA: 1996. n.p. Print.

"Wipers steady," "Home at last," "Night Falls" [corrected version]. *Frogpond* 19.1. New York: Haiku Society of America, 1996. 8, 20, 52. Print.

"Innocent Diversions" *Chain* 3. *Special Topic: Hybrid Genres/Mixed Media.* Buffalo: 1996. 183-188. Print.

"Night falls," *Woodnotes* 28. [Associate Editor: Gail Sher]. Foster City, CA, Spring 1996. 9. Print.

"The boy dozes," "Winter sun." *Woodnotes* 29 [Associate Editor: Gail Sher]. Foster City, CA, Summer, 1996. 10, 22. Print.

"George Tooker: Marginalia" [excerpt]. *Big Allis* 7. Brooklyn: 1996. 30-33. Print.

"Autumn leaves." *Ant* 3: *A Periodical of Autochthonous Poetry & Other Conundrums.* Oakland, CA, Summer 1996. n.p. Print.

"Resurrection," "The Seven Sacraments." *Raddle Moon* 15. Vancouver, BC, Canada, 1996. 113-118. Print.

"Noisy city." *Raw NerVZ* 2.4. Aylmer, QC, Canada: Proof Press, Winter 1995-96. 29. Print.

"Winds blow briskly this evening." *Five Lines Down: A Tanka Journal.* Redwood City, CA: Winter 1995. 12. Print.

"Even in his company," "The wind blows stronger." *Woodnotes,* 25. San Francisco: Haiku Poets of Northern California, Summer 1995. 8, 13. Print.

"Cross-legged I sit." *Ant* 2. Oakland, CA: Summer 1995. n.p. Print.

"Home at last" [includes Japanese translation]. *Basho Festival Dedicatory Anthology.* [Award]. Ueno City, Mie Prefecture, Japan: Master Basho Museum, 1995. n.p. Print.

"Night falls." *Woodnotes* 26. San Francisco: Haiku Poets of Northern California, Autumn 1995. 24. Print.

"Snow buries," "A train whistle blows," "Tassajara Summer 1969." *Woodnotes* 27. San Francisco: Haiku Poets of Northern California, Winter 1995. 17, 31, 41. Print.

"Folding its wings." *Modern Haiku,* 26.1. Madison, WI: 1995. 10. Print.

"Sudden squall," "Misty rain." *Frogpond* 18.3. New York, NY: Haiku Society of America, Autumn 1995. 22, 37. Print.

"Night Falls." *Frogpond* 18.4. New York, NY: Haiku Society of America, Winter 1995. 21. Print.

"Silent snow." *Woodnotes* 23. San Francisco: Haiku Poets of Northern California, Winter 1994. 5. Print.

"la" [excerpt]. *Big Allis* 5. New York, 1992. 34-41. Print.

"Ex voto" [excerpt from *Broke Aide* (1985) translated into French by Pierre Alferi & Joseph Simas]. *49+1: Nouveaux Poètes Américains.* Eds. Emmanuel Hocquard & Claude Royet-Journoud. Royaumont (France): 1991. 222-223. Print.

"Osiris co rider" [from "Kuklos"]. *Gallery Works* 8. Aptos, CA: 1991. n.p. Print.

"Tamarind Esau" [from "Kuklos"]. *Big Allis* 1. New York: 1989. Print.

"W/" *Abacus* 35. Elmwood, CT: Potes & Poets Press: 1988. n.p. Print.

"The Fasting Spirit." [review essay on anorexia nervosa, with excerpts from "Moon of the Swaying Buds"]. *The San Francisco Jung Institute Library Journal,* 8:2. San Francisco: 1988. 61-80. Print.

*Starving passion: A Tribute to Anorexia.* Thesis (M.A.), John F. Kennedy University, 1988, listed in: catalog.jfku.edu; print copy in the Gail Sher Collection, Poetry Collection, University at Buffalo.

"Cops" [excerpt read by Gail Sher at UCSD November 24, 1987]. *Archive Newsletter: The Archive of New Poetry.* San Diego: University of California, 1987. 12-14. Print.

"Cops" [excerpt]. *Writing* 18. Vancouver BC, Canada: 1987. Print.

Ten poems. *Gallery Works* 7. Norwalk, CT: 1987. n.p. Print.

"For Bart II." *Karamu,* 10:2. Charleston, IL: Eastern Illinois University, 1987. 14-19. Print.

"The Lanyard." *Notus: New Writing,* 1:1. Ann Arbor: 1986. 13-21. Print.

"For Bart." *Tramen,* 4. San Francisco: 1985. n.p. Print.

"Which Collateral Bends the Sea," "Deft and Resilient." *Gallery Works* 6. Bronx, NY: 1984. n.p. Print.

Poems. *Credences: A Journal of Twentieth Century Poetry and Poetics,* New Series 3:1. Buffalo: State University of New York, 1984. 84-88. Print.

"From Another Point of View the Woman Seems To Be Resting." *Credences: A Journal of Twentieth Century Poetry and Poetics,* New Series 2:1, Buffalo: State University of New York, 1982. 9-11. Print.

"Suppose deeply offers up." *Hambone* 2. Santa Cruz, CA, 1982. 18-22. Print.

"River the Office My Own," "Lord and Give the Necklace Child" *Gallery Works* 5. Bronx, NY: 1981.n.p. Print.

Poems. *Gnome Baker* 7 & 8 (1981): n.p. [10 pages]. Print.

Nine Pieces. *Credences: A Journal of Twentieth Century Poetry and Poetics,* New Series 1:1, Buffalo: University at Buffalo, 1981. 16-20. Print.

"foal the water bush." *Hoots Who*. San Francisco: Boiled Owl, 1980. n.p. Print.

"An Exorcism of Representational Language" [review of *Red Light with Blue Sky* by Beau Beausoleil]. L=A=N=G=U=A=G=E 11. New York, January 1980. n.p. Print.

# Resources

The *Gail Sher Digital Collection* in the Poetry Collection of the Univeristy at Buffalo contains downloadable copies of almost all of Gail Sher's poetry books and journal appearances as well as audio and video recordings of interviews, readings, and discussions.
digital.lib.buffalo.edu/collection/LIB-PC011/

The *Gail Sher Collection* in the Poetry Collection of the University at Buffalo includes manuscripts, notebooks, correspondence, photographs, artwork, documentation of her published work, and many of the journals in which her poetry appeared.
findingaids.lib.buffalo.edu/repositories/3/resources/572

*Gail Sher Poetry & Poetics 1980-2020*
is set in Minion, a digital typeface designed by
Robert Slimbach in the spirit of the humanist
typefaces of fifteenth-century Venice;
it was released by Adobe Systems in 1990
Cover Design: Bryan Kring
Cover Art: Gail Sher

www.ingramcontent.com/pod-product-compliance
Lightning Source LLC
Chambersburg PA
CBHW070408100426
42812CB00005B/1674